NAMMA
BANGALORE

Shoba Narayan is the author of five books. She has been a journalist and columnist for 30 years, writing about travel, food, wine, culture, crafts and relationships, for national and international publications. She has won a James Beard Award and a Pulitzer Fellowship. She has taught and lectured at universities in India and abroad.

She is interested in Indian aesthetics, and has researched its influence on jewellery, music, textiles and scents. She founded and co-created a website called *Project LooM*, which documents the weaving traditions of India. She is a birdwatcher, wine-drinker and gadget geek. Her lifelong mission is to get fit without exercising and lose weight without dieting.

NAMMA
BANGALORE

THE SOUL OF A METROPOLIS

SHOBA NARAYAN

RUPA

Published by
Rupa Publications India Pvt. Ltd 2023
7/16, Ansari Road, Daryaganj
New Delhi 110002

Sales centres:
Bengaluru Chennai Hyderabad
Jaipur Kathmandu Kolkata
Mumbai Prayagraj

Some parts of this book were first published by HT Media and Condé Nast.

The views and opinions expressed in this book are the author's own and the facts are as reported by her which have been verified to the extent possible, and the publishers are not in any way liable for the same.

P-ISBN: 978-93-5702-466-2
E-ISBN: 978-93-5702-478-5

First impression 2023

10 9 8 7 6 5 4 3 2 1

The moral right of the author has been asserted.

Printed in India

For
Shyam, Priya, Sangeeta and Harsha,
who made Bangalore home for us

∞

Contents

Introduction

Bangalore is home. I didn't always live here. I grew up in Chennai and lived in New York and Singapore before moving to Bangalore in 2005. But Bangalore is the city where my kids grew up. They call it 'home' and return here for holidays. This is where I hail autorickshaws for bone-rattling yet perversely exciting rides to work and meetings; where I prowl pubs and malls in search of stories and sales; where I go to Thom's Bakery & Supermarket to buy bread, beer and, on occasion, brownies.

It turns out that Bangalore, the capital of Karnataka, is also home to a growing number of immigrants from other states within India as well as expats who work for Citibank, General Electric, Honeywell, Philips, Texas Instruments and hundreds of other multinationals. The numbers are small compared with, say, Hong Kong, but since the late 1990s, foreigners have thronged Bangalore at a rate that alarmed the locals, who were used to their sleepy town being called 'pensioner's paradise'.

'Are we being Bangalored in Bangalore?' goes the line, alluding to the growing number of local jobs being taken by foreigners.

Besides the foreigners who live and work in Bangalore, thousands fly in every day for meetings and conferences or to clinch a deal. They stay at one of the city's pricey hotels, savour its pubs, buy sandalwood oil and silk scarves and drive to Electronic City for their meetings. In fact, if you only take in the glass-and-steel high-rises of South Bangalore and ignore the beggars, flower sellers, squeegee men, vegetable vendors and holy cows, it is possible to imagine that you are driving through California's Silicon Valley. The banners on buildings come quick and bold—Cisco Systems, Google, Hewlett–Packard, Microsoft, Sun Microsystems, Yahoo—and, together, they give this city its rather uninspired moniker: India's Silicon Valley. This book is written in part for these foreigners who fly into Bangalore for meetings and visits.

A Word About Names

Although most Bangaloreans call the city by its colonial name, Bangalore, we are still getting used to our city's new official name— Bengaluru. In fact, when my editor suggested 'Namma Bangalore' as the title of this book, I told him that it should be 'Namma Bengaluru' because that is how it was said. But we both realized that when people search online for books on Bangalore, they type 'Bangalore' and not 'Bengaluru', which put us in on the horns of a dilemma. *Namma Bangalore was a compromise.*

In this book, I use both Bengaluru and Bangalore interchangeably, depending on the cadence of the sentence. Mostly, I use 'Bangalore', although I hope that we all soon call this place 'Bengaluru'. It sounds better and goes well with the Kannada name for the city. I also love the new official city logo that is a mix of English and Kannada.

The Garden City

Unlike Silicon Valley, Bangalore is not a valley. It squats atop the Precambrian Deccan Plateau, at approximately 3,000 ft above sea level (about the same elevation as Caracas). Winter temperatures rarely drop below 15°C; and even the two hottest months of the year—April and May—see average temperatures only in the high 20s. Bangalore's temperate weather is its biggest boon and the reason why so many returning Indians, including me, choose to live here. It is like living in perpetual New York spring, replete with thousands of flowering trees.

The men who were responsible for making Bangalore India's

'Garden City' by planting the trees we see today were a sultan and a German. The first, Hyder Ali, who ruled the Deccan Plateau in the eighteenth century, was apparently so taken by the Mughal Gardens in Delhi that he resolved to duplicate them. In 1760, he set aside 240 acres for the Lalbagh or Red Garden, named for its roses, and planted trees from all over the world. Emissaries from foreign lands were encouraged to bring plants as gifts. Today, Lalbagh is a thriving park with 200-year-old trees, three-billion-year-old rock formations, dog walkers, joggers and members of Bangalore's many laughter clubs—senior citizens who get together every morning just to giggle and guffaw.

It was a German horticulturist and his able deputy who took Hyder Ali's vision to near-poetic heights. Handpicked by Maharaja Krishnaraja Wadiyar IV to landscape the palace gardens, Gustav Hermann Krumbiegel and H.C. Javaraya left their stamp all over Bangalore. It was Krumbiegel's idea to flank the boulevards with sequentially flowering trees. The website *Wild Wanderer* gives the entire list of flowering trees in order: red silk-cotton trees blooming in January, orange silver oak in February, purple jacaranda in March, pink cassia in April, rain trees in May, gulmohar trees in June, nagalinga or canonball trees in July and, indeed, throughout the year, spathodea in August, Colville's glory in October, *Millingtonia hortensis* or akash mallige trees in November and pink and yellow tabebuias in December. And I have not even mentioned the bauhinias, ashokas and flowering fig trees that dot Bangalore's boulevards.

Bangaloreans are passionate gardeners and proud tree huggers. Some years ago, Prem Koshy, the owner of Koshy's Café, where the city's literati meet and argue over open toast sandwiches and coffee, created a stir by climbing up a mahogany tree outside his restaurant and refusing to come down till the government promised not to cut it down. The tree still arches over St Mark's Road and Koshy distributes mahogany seeds to his customers.

The Scent of Bangalore

The best writing on scent comes from the late Palestinian poet Mahmoud Darwish, who writes not about the scent of a woman or a man but about the scent of cities. His writing is so evocative that I am compelled to quote it:

> Cities are smells—Accra is the smell of iodine and spices. Haifa is the smell of pine and wrinkled sheets. Moscow is the smell of vodka on ice. Cairo is the smell of mango and ginger. Beirut is the smell of the sun, sea, smoke and lemons. Paris is the smell of fresh bread, cheese and derivations of enchantment. Damascus is the smell of jasmine and dried fruit. Tunis is the smell of night musk and salt. Rabat is the smell of henna, incense and honey. A city that cannot be known by its smell is unreliable.[1]

I disagree with Darwish, even though I love his writing. Damascus is the scent of luscious roses, not jasmine. The best jasmine comes from Tamil Nadu, in my view. But 'cities are smells', as Darwish said.

Delhi is the smell of garam masala, wealth and fetid desire. Mumbai is the smell of speed (not the drug, but the verb), sea and petrol fumes. Pune is the smell of *goda* masala and *tanpuras*. Kolkata is the smell of fish, *addas* and sweat. Jaipur is the scent of wafting veils, pearls, chiffon and *kachori*. Amritsar is the scent of langar, parathas and service. Vadodara is the smell of banyan, *baithaks* and artist's oil paint. As for Bangalore...Bangalore is the smell of red earth and falling rain; of open drains and clogged leaves; of start-ups and *swalpa adjust maadi* (please adjust).

It is the scent of sweat and enterprise that seeps through the skin, mingled with spices and cigar smoke—occasionally unpleasant but certainly unmistakable.

---

[1]Darwish, Mahmoud, 'Mahmoud Darwish: What is Lost', *Pen America*, 29 February 2012, https://tinyurl.com/4erah9ej. Accessed on 15 June 2023.

Scents evoke a sigh, sometimes a wistful one. Sometimes they evoke a quick inhalation of surprise and desire. Even if you cannot vocalize it, a funny thing will happen when you drive through Bangalore—you will roll down your car's windows, smell something from far away and think of the woman that got away. A scent is a memory. Sometimes it reminds us of the people we love, and sometimes, of the ones that got away.

In that sense, Bangalore is a place that is hard to get away from. Most people come here and rarely leave.

THE METROPOLIS

Well, Not Just a Metropolis

In my view, Bangalore is India's most genteel metropolis. It disdains Delhi's nouveau riche ostentation and Mumbai's spunky shrewdness. It isn't as conservative as neighbouring Chennai and is more cosmopolitan than Hyderabad.

Bangaloreans have a grace and gentility to them that years of frenzied moneymaking have not erased. Some say that this is because of a congenital inability to say 'no' to a request. This is sometimes difficult for residents such as me. Plumbers promise to come over right away to fix leaking pipes when they are stuck in traffic and know they can't. Carpenters assert that they can build modular cabinets when they are, in fact, skilled carvers. But this intent to accommodate, however misguided and frustrating, lubricates life for tourists. Most people smile and say 'yes' to a request—any request. The pace of the city is slow. Most shops open at 10.00 a.m., sometimes at 10.30 a.m. Restaurants, even the good ones (and there are many of these), don't insist on turning tables. If you want to linger, nobody is going to hustle you out. In Bangalore, I can hail a cab or an autorickshaw without haggling over the fare. Sure, there is the traffic, but the honks are milder than, say, Boston or Bombay. People don't curse or swear in public; flipping the middle finger is a useless gesture—nobody does these things here. And there are enough big companies to guarantee or at least attempt private-public participation. Kiran Mazumdar Shaw, one of India's richest women, began her company, Biocon, in a garage here. A brew master-turned-biotechnologist, Shaw is a civic activist and often speaks out about Bangalore's infrastructure and pollution woes.

Part of Bangalore's economic success comes from a long tradition of welcoming immigrants. The city was established as a British army cantonment. Former British Prime Minister Winston Churchill served here in his youth and owed ₹13 to the Bangalore Club. King Charles, then prince, offered to settle the account when he visited Bangalore in the late 1980s, but the Club, which proudly displays young Churchill's outstanding dues in its ledger, refused. Christians and Muslims from neighbouring states came to cook and serve the army. Later, the information technology (IT) boom attracted savvy North Indians, who took up assignments and ended up staying. Most Indians feel at home here, whether they speak Kannada or not.

Like the rest of India, Bangalore contradicts itself all the time. It lives in many centuries, marrying the traditional with the modern. Bangalore's burgeoning wealth has also spawned trends that are more typical of developed economies. I suffer power cuts but get organic vegetables delivered to my home every week. Civic sense is sporadic but one small boutique—Daily Dump—designs and sells terracotta composting pots as if to leapfrog the garbage on the streets. Jobs are so intense that few claim to have the time to read, and yet the city has four local newspapers. Second-hand bookstores abound. The civic infrastructure is under constant threat of collapse, but there are an astonishing number of eco-friendly buildings with solar panels and rainwater harvesting systems. The roads are potholed, and yet one of them will take you to Soukya, a world-class holistic health centre, built on 30 acres, that has attracted the likes of King Charles, Tina Turner and Archbishop Desmond Tutu. Many youngsters work in fluorescent call centres all night but go rock-climbing, hiking and mountain biking during the day in the rocky terrain surrounding Bangalore. In fact, *Sholay*, a legendary Bollywood film about dacoits and thieves, was shot in Ramanagara, a rocky outcrop that is an hour away from Bangalore. Beer is the beverage of choice and pubs are prolific, and yet, the Bangalore Wine Club (BWC) meets once a month to sample wines from around the world and pontificate on the state of Indian wines, particularly Grover's, whose vineyards are two hours away. Café Coffee Day (CCD), India's answer to Starbucks, was started here.

Women can wear Western clothes and not feel out of place in this progressive city. It is also safe to hire taxis and autorickshaws; the drivers are honest and use a meter to record the fare. Sure, there is the traffic, so one must always factor in extra time when going from meeting to meeting.

You come to Bangalore to sell a dream and create a start-up. This wasn't a part of Bangalore's founding history but it will be a part of its future.

Is Bangalore India's 'Idea' City?

Search for India's start-up capital and two cities come up—Bangalore and Delhi. Recently, there has been some rather unwarranted talk about Delhi pipping Bangalore as the top contender for this position. I would like to submit that this is just plain wrong. Delhi can never equal Bangalore in the start-up ecosystem for one simple reason—Delhi's traffic can never be as bad as Bangalore's.

I can just see all the Mumbaikars shaking their heads, thinking, *You poor child. You ain't seen traffic till you've been on Marine Drive during rush hour.*

Dilliwallahs, too, can offer sturdy competition. *We have more VVIPs than you Bangaloreans*, they will say. *You have no idea of how our traffic stalls when a minister goes by.*

In response to all these claims, we Bangaloreans will just take another bite of our *maddur vada* and spit-laugh in your faces. Mumbai's traffic jams are limited to certain locations, Delhi's to certain times. However, Bangalore has traffic jams all the time at all locations. Our traffic snarls up for no rhyme or reason. Just like Bangalore has elements of spring, summer, monsoon and winter all within one day, we also have traffic jams of multiple types at different points during the day. And that, ladies and gentlemen, is our secret sauce for creating 'unicorns'. Yes, you heard me right. We not only have the biggest, hairiest and the best traffic jams but we also embrace them because they contribute to our start-up ecosystem—they are the reason we have 'unicorns', a term coined by venture capitalist Aileen Lee to describe a start-up company which has a value of over $1 billion.

Imagine the average start-up founder sitting in a car in Bangalore. He (or occasionally, she) is en route to a meeting, and traffic is, as always, stalled. So what does he do? He checks his messages, emails, Instagram and then, defeated, looks out of the window to see if the traffic is inching along. Exhausted, he stares at the rain trees all around. Eureka! He gets an idea of how to solve the knotty vendor issue.

It is a well-known fact that the brain needs downtime in order to come up with creative ideas. Newton was half-napping when he discovered gravity. Archimedes was in a bathtub when he came up with the Archimedes's principle. Bangalore's traffic provides excellent downtime for entrepreneurs and founders to come up with life-changing ideas.

More than Delhi or any other city in India, Bangalore is a city of ideas. I am not the only person saying this. Worthier folks predate me in saying this.

Technocrat and entrepreneur Nandan Nilekani is not sure whether he came up with the idea of calling Bangalore a 'city of ideas', but he is pretty sure he was one of the earliest to do so. 'Nehru said it before me,' he admits.[1]

Jawaharlal Nehru said a lot more during his address at Bangalore's Vidhana Soudha in July 1962. But essentially, he called Bangalore 'the city of the future'.

'Now Bangalore, in many ways, is unlike the other great cities of India,' said our late prime minister. Most of the other great Indian cities were mired in the past, present and future, but mostly, the past. 'Bangalore, however, presented India a picture of the future, because of the concentration of science, technology and industries in the public sector here,' said Nehru.

That remains unchanged even after 60 years. In his speech, Nehru advises how to preserve the forward-thinking nature of one of India's 'most beautiful' cities. All of this can be read in

---

[1]'The (Applied) Ideas Man', *Shoba Narayan*, https://tinyurl.com/5843ymmf. Accessed on 1 May 2023.

M. Fazlul Hasan's excellent book *Bangalore through the Centuries.*[2]

Nehru saw in Bangalore the existence of two major incentives of good life—civic sense and aesthetic consciousness. You can question whether the latter still exists, now that metro construction, potholed roads and horrible traffic have changed the aesthetics of this city. But civic action is still strong. Protests remain pervasive and citizens queue up to safeguard lakes, trees and green spaces.

'In the future, Bangalore may acquire such appellations as "Industrial City", "Prosperous City" or "Thriving City",' said our late prime minister.[3]

Clearly, Nehru was preaching to the gallery with respect to his monikers for Bangalore. There are other cities in India that can vie for the title of being the most industrial, prosperous or thriving, but when it comes to being an 'idea city', Bangalore, I would argue, is peerless. This is where Nilekani comes in.

Nilekani's view is similar, but he calls Bangalore a city 'of ideas'. He said this when I profiled him for *Mint Lounge* in 2007:

> Delhi is mired in the past. It was the seat of some seven different empires all of whom wanted to project power. Mumbai, even today, is India's seat of commerce, finance, and economy. Bangalore lives for tomorrow. It is about ideas and change, partly because the locals are benign and welcoming towards people from all over the world. Bangaloreans, on the whole, are forward-looking people.[4]

Plus, our traffic jams help us ruminate, masticate, digest and deliver on ideas.

[2]Hasan, M. Fazlul, *Bangalore Through the Centuries*, Historical Publications, California, 1970.
[3]Ibid.
[4]'Bangalore Talkies: Why Bangalore's Traffic Makes It the Startup Capital of India?', *Shoba Narayan*, https://tinyurl.com/264me5wf. Accessed on 1 May 2023.

How to Spot a Bangalorean

There is a face that a Bangalorean will make when you ask him to do something. It is a contortion, almost comical in its sincerity. It says, 'What you are asking for is currently difficult for me but I really want to accommodate and help you. So please help me help you—by downsizing your expectations, if possible to zero. Then we can just get along and have a By2 coffee together.'

As an honorary Bangalorean, I have spotted this face often—in plumbers and mechanics, sales managers and saree-sellers. It comes out when you urgently need something and they need to have their *oota*, *kaapi* or *thindi* (lunch, coffee or tiffin, respectively). I have made this face when someone asks me for a favour—to buy time, to say no without really saying 'no'. It is a face with a hand gesture that seems like you are grasping a lotus by the stem and a look that says, 'Swalpa adjust maadi.'

Bangaloreans do this often without drama or fuss. We take things in our stride. If you give us *jolada rotti* (*jowar* or sorghum roti), we will eat it. Ragi *mudde* (ragi balls), you say? We will swallow it. *Akki rotti* (rice roti)? Heck yes. We will enjoy it fully, especially if it has *sabsige soppu* or dill leaves. The point is that every Bangalorean savours the moment, is grateful for what is given, doesn't make a fuss, tries to cultivate humility and lives life to the fullest.

You can see it in the way we stand outside tiny roadside hotels, taking small bites of our vadas and chatting quietly with each other as the morning sunshine filters through the gently swaying rain trees. You can see it in Airlines Hotel, where we sit under the young morning sun and take long, slow sips of our coffee from glass tumblers, trying to prolong the beauty of the moment.

Road rage is minimal here even though the traffic snarls. Sure, the Uttara Karnataka or 'UK' folks have fire in their veins and are known for their slang and swear words—all of which come out fluently and have exact correlations with their Hindi counterparts. What do you think *soole maga* or *baddi maga* mean?

But even the firebrands from other regions of Karnataka and other states calm down when they come to Bangalore. Why is that? For a city of some 13 million, Bangaloreans are amongst the most genteel and polite people in India, if not the world. Ours is not the formal politeness of certain cultures. Our gentility comes from within. Why? We don't know the answer ourselves.

Perhaps, it has to do with the weather. Every day here is like April in Paris, complete with blooming flowers and trees, no matter where you go. The living is easy, and not just 'in the summertime', to quote the popular jazz song.

The other reason for the Bangalorean's ability to adapt and adjust is because Karnataka is perhaps more diverse than most other states. We have practice in getting along with a variety of folks.

First, there is coastal Karnataka or Tulu Nadu with its distinctive Tulu language, culture and rituals like *bhoota kola*, made famous by the movie *Kantara*. Coastal Karnataka and Mangalore (now Mangaluru) are melting pots of India's three big faiths. While, Mangalorean Christians seem to have music in their bones, it's the cuisine of the Konkani Muslims that is distinct and delicious and stands out. As for the Hindus, they too have their quirks and foibles that you can read about in translated books such as *Defiance* by Na Mogasale.

Then there is Coorg, famous for its language and customs, its beauteous landscape, handsome people, its nature worship that reveres the river Kaveri and its famous *pandi* curry made with pork.

Upper Karnataka, with its dry drought-laden landscape, plain-speaking, freely-swearing and earthy people, is the stuff of legend in the state. Ironically, for such a barren land, its people are amongst the most cultured. Hubli–Dharwad is home to Gangubai Hangal, Mallikarjun Mansur, D.R. Bendre and Leena Chandavarkar. It is home to the Dharwad *pedha*, Gokak *karadhantu*, Ladagi laddu, Belagavi *kunda*, Tuppada *mandige* and many other sweets.

There is also the Udupi and Kundapur heartland with its own dialect, customs, spice mixes and famous dishes including the Kundapur *koli saaru* or chicken gravy, Udupi sambhar and other delicacies. The masala dosa was invented in Udupi.

The Mysuru–Mandya region brings its own ecosystem with its sugarcane fields, Mysore *pak*, Mysore masala dosa, Mysore *bonda* and Mysore Concerns Coffee that is now famous in Mumbai's Matunga.

Given this mishmash of locals, it is no wonder that the average Bangalorean needs to 'adjust'. Add to this, immigrants like me, from states far and near. Everyone somehow jostles through and gets along. Some part of this is the reflexive politeness of the native Kannadiga. The people who keep talking about Lucknow's *tehzeeb* have not met the average Kannadiga.

Here's an example. There is this story that goes around in the IAS (Indian Adminstrative Services) circles of Bangalore, about how a peon shows his new boss around the office. 'And here, Sir, is your kind office, your kind chair, and the next room is the kind bathroom and the kind commode,' he says. It sounds better in the bureaucratic Kannada accent mixed with English. Go to Bangalore Club and get your IAS old-timer friends to down a local beer or two and ask them to recount this story to get the full picture, complete with a deferential posture.

It is this gentility that is part of the Bangalorean DNA. No matter where you are from, you will fit in and get along with people here. The autorickshaw driver will speak your language of choice—whether it is Telugu or Tamil. The courier delivery person will offer to speak in Hindi if you look North Indian before realizing that you can speak Kannada. The policeman will say a few words in English if he senses that your Kannada is bad.

In which other Indian city can you see this happening?

10 Mind-Blowing Things about Bangalore's History

There is a persistent narrative that Bangalore is a new city, compared not just to North Indian cities like Delhi that flaunt their histories but also to neighbouring ones like Chennai or Hyderabad. Bangalore is often dismissed as India's Silicon Valley that morphed from a sleepy pensioner's paradise and garden city. The other popular stereotypes about Bangalore are that it is a cosmopolitan and fast-growing city—which are both true. But most people don't think of this city as ancient, even though it is. Bangalore is a city where the truly ancient and the truly modern coexist.

'All over Bangalore, you can find inscriptions, some that date back to as early as 517 CE,' says Udaya Kumar P.L., who calls himself a citizen historian but is in fact an expert in the history of Bangalore. He points out various areas in Bangalore that are decidedly ancient—Indiranagar, now known for its pubs, is over 1,000 years old. The same is true for J.P. Nagar, Domlur, Marathahalli—all of which we associate with traffic snarls and unhinged development.

Heritage buffs abound in this city and many of them follow Uday, who is interested in epigraphy, inscriptions, temples, hero stones and pretty much anything old. I met Uday a few years ago, when he showed me a 'hero stone' or *veera gallu* in Hebbal, which, if you know Bangalore, is among the most congested areas in the city. This particular hero stone, discovered in a roadside ditch, had inscriptions dating back to 750 CE. It commemorated the valour of one Hebbal-Kittayya, who was martyred while defending an attack on his village. 'He is the first Bangalorean whose name we know and so many of us call him "Bangalore's first citizen",' says Uday.

I called Uday recently to find out some other amazing things about this city. Uday gave me a list of things that every person who is interested in Bangalore should know. The list given below is based on original research findings that Uday and his team who volunteer at The Mythic Society of Bangalore have discovered. They can be accessed when you visit The Mythic Society on Nrupathunga Road.

1. Bangalore is linked to the earth's beginning. Some 3.5 billion years ago, the Dharwar Craton, now considered the oldest part of the Indian peninsula, was formed. Below the Dharwar Craton was the equally old Peninsular Gneiss. The beauty is that you can see this Precambrian rock in Lalbagh. When you climb up the Lalbagh rock, you are standing on a formation that is 3.5 billion years old.

2. Roman coins have been found in Bangalore. In 1965, while constructing a runway at the old Hindustan Aeronautics Limited (HAL) airport, a pot containing 256 Roman silver coins was found. Much earlier in 1891, while constructing a railway line in Yeshwantpur, 163 Roman silver coins, including ones bearing the faces of Augustus, Tiberius and Claudius were discovered. The Roman Empire fell in 476 CE, so imagine finding 1,700-year-old coins in the heart of Bangalore!

3. The oldest Bangalore-related inscription goes back to 517 CE, in an area close to today's infamous Silk Board junction, called Begur. Abutting Begur Lake is the Panchalingeshwara Temple that dates back to 1100 CE. It is the oldest temple in South India—older than the ones in Thanjavur, Madurai and Andhra Pradesh. Here, in a 900 CE inscription, the name given to our city is 'BeMgUlurA'. Interestingly, Andhra Pradesh State Road Transport Corporation (APSRTC) buses still spell the name

as 'BengUlurA', not the currently flipped around spelling and pronunciation of 'BengAlurU'.

4. These inscriptions prove that the fanciful folktale about how Bangalore got its name is wrong. The story goes that a twelfth-century Hoysala king, called Vira Ballala II, lost his way during a hunt. An old woman offered the tired king some boiled beans. The king in royal fashion christened the area '*Benda-kaalu–ooru*', which means the town of boiled beans. The tale is terrific but patently false.

5. The man who found the Begur inscription, R. Narasimhachar, a former director at the Directorate of Archaeology and Museums, Mysore has written in the Mysore Archaeological Survey's report of 1915, [...] the inscription testifies to the antiquity of Bengaluru, the modern Bangalore, which must have existed under this name in about 900 CE. We may now discard the story of Vira Ballala (1173–1220) having gone to the hut of an old woman and eaten *bengalu* (boiled beans)[...][5]

6. What people think of as the oldest parts of the city are actually the youngest and vice versa. Chickpete, Balepete and their neighbouring areas are relatively young. In contrast, Indiranagar has inscriptions dating back to 1200 CE. They were found at the Binna Mangala bus stand which still exists.

7. Similarly, Domlur has the beautiful Chokkanathaswamy temple that goes back 1,000 years. The same with J.P. Nagar, Marathahalli, Malleshwaram and many others—all of which have inscription stones that are centuries old.

8. Inscription stones are carved writing in stones, usually documenting something significant—a donation to build a temple, tank or community centre. It is often a record of public goods or grants given by a king. 'It is like the 80G receipts of today, except the donation is forever,' says Uday. About 175 inscription stones have been discovered in Bangalore, out

---

[5]'The Quarter That Was', *Intacher*, Vol. 2, No. 1, 2019, p. 1, https://tinyurl.com/s3k75j23. Accessed on 30 April 2023.

of which only 110 are traceable today. The remainder were destroyed, mostly due to real estate construction.

9. All of Bangalore's famous lakes are man-made. Ulsoor Lake and Sankey Tank are the youngest lakes. Bellandur Lake, with its soapy overload, is 2,000 years old, as are Begur and Hebbal lakes. We know this because Durga idols have been found near these lakes. Traditionally, Durga idols, along with Ganesha and Kshetrapalaka idols, were built to safeguard lakes.

10. Those interested in the history of the region should watch a video on YouTube called 'Journey of Bangalore—Southern Hemisphere till 15th Century', put out by Mythic Society Media. Those who would like to get involved in documenting the inscription stones in Bangalore can join a Facebook group called 'Inscription Stones of Bangalore'.

So you see, don't dismiss this city as merely modern. Bangalore is as modern and cosmopolitan as it gets, but, at the same time, it is also an ancient settlement.

What Makes Bangalore Special?

Among those who live and love their cities—and the two don't necessarily go together—there is often a somewhat trite parlour-game that is played, usually after copious amounts of alcohol. The game relates to identity—of a city and a person. It often begins with the question: are you a true Bangalorean? If the participants can manage to keep away the needless competition that springs up ('my city is better than yours!'), the game can actually make you figure out the essence of your city and yourself. What makes your city different from other cities? Who is a true Parisienne, Mumbaikar, New Yorker or Bangalorean? In an age of global migration, is this question even relevant?

Well, a good place to start would be language and lineage. A true Bangalorean has lived in the city over generations and speaks the local language. As with any definition, the exceptions define the contours of this debate, and especially so in Bangalore. Go to Chickpete or Avenue Road and you will find third-generation Marwaris who sell silver vessels and handwoven silk sarees. Go to Ulsoor and you will find Mudaliars from Chennai whose ancestors came to Bangalore to work for the British and who now own vast tracts of land. Both communities speak Kannada and have lived here for generations. But they choose their spouses from within their own community, defining themselves in this key life-choice as outsiders.

A better question is: what type of a Bangalorean are you?

I will list out a few types of Bangalore and you can see if you relate to any of them.

There is the Bangalore of Cubbon Park and Lalbagh, filled with birdwatchers, runners, forest-bathers and tree-huggers—all of whom repair to these arbours every day or at least every weekend, for their fill of oxygen and exercise. These informal groups used to end their exertions with a coffee from a *darshini* (small restaurant) or MTR (Mavalli Tiffin Rooms); although locals would say that both Vidyarthi Bhavan and MTR are overrated. Today, in the age of intermittent fasting, these groups 'cheat' by scarfing down the best *vada pav* outside Mumbai from the street vendor who stands near the entrance of Cubbon Park.

Wildlife is a big theme amongst Bangaloreans, situated as we are, hours from the Nilgiri Biosphere. On Telegram, there are approximately 10 groups devoted to this topic—Bangalore Wildlife Friends, Nature Conservation Group, Bangalore Butterfly Club, Project Gubbi Goodu that makes nest-boxes for birds and many others. Join one of these groups and you will meet experts on arachnids, moths, ants or bats.

If you are a foodie, Facebook is your quickest route to connect with food lovers in Bangalore. There are large groups with 182,000 members and smaller specific ones like the Cooke Town Foodies, Bangalore Coffee Thindi and Oota Club. There is a Koramangala Lunch Group (KLG) that meets every week. There are also several wine and single malt groups that focus on the tipple rather than the dish. But all great Indian cities have such food and wine groups. What then is specific and special to Bangalore?

Is it our love for bookstores like Blossom or cafés like Koshy's, both of which have a sense of place and authenticity that are hard to duplicate? Is it the elderly aunties and uncles who wander in the by-lanes of Malleswaram and Basavanagudi, bargaining for vegetables and praying at the Bull Temple? Is it the churches that dot the 'Cantt side' or cantonment side of Bangalore, each with their own ethos and attracting the faithful for sermons, or in my case, midnight mass on Christmas eve? Is it Mosque Road where all of Bangalore seems to congregate during Ramadan for *haleem*?

I could be wrong but fashion is not a part of Bangalore's

mojo, not because we don't have talent but because even rich Bangaloreans have a frugality relative to, say, Delhites.

The performing arts thrive here, with theatres like Jagriti, Rangashankara, Gayana Samaja, Seva Sadan and Chowdiah Hall. India's major dance forms, including Bharatanatyam, Kathak and Odissi have practitioners here. Karnataka is at the crossroads of music, both Hindustani and Carnatic. This state is home to both Gangubai Hangal and M.L. Vasanthakumari. Art and art galleries don't attract as many patrons as they do in, say, Mumbai, but that may change in the coming years.

So what makes Bangalore different? Is it our love of comedy and comedians such as Aiyyo Shraddha, Danish Sait, Pushpavalli and Aporup Acharya who make us laugh? Is it the 'adjust maadi' spirit that helps this city jog along? Is it the city's golf courses—two within city limits and several outside it? (Friends from Chennai come here for the weekend just to play golf.)

Ultimately, I came up with the one thing that makes Bangalore special—you know where I am heading, right? It is that most tired cliché of all—the weather. Come April, when everyone flees to the hills, Bangalore is balmy. Through the year, weather is a non-issue and is never discussed. We don't have bad hair days. At all. And that, for any city, is special.

One of my favourite Twitter posts last year was the following: 'Hey Bangaloreans, is everything all right? Nobody has boasted about your city's weather in the last 24 hours.'

To Learn Kannada or Not:
That Is the Question

Why do so few outsiders bother to learn Kannada? I know North Indians who have lived here for 30 years. Ask them if they speak Kannada and they shake their heads. Some try to explain their choice by saying that they haven't found the need; after all, everyone in Bangalore speaks Hindi. The same logic applies to Telugu and Tamil people who settle and thrive in Bangalore for decades without learning Kannada.

Compare this to Chennai, where I grew up. It was unthinkable for anyone to speak anything other than Tamil on the streets. Cab and autorickshaw drivers would only speak Tamil and turn snarky, rude or disparaging if you spoke anything else. Shopkeepers would openly mock you if you didn't speak the language and then proceed to take you for a ride since they knew you were not a local.

Hyderabad was different. Both Hindi and Telugu ruled the street. In Kerala, everyone not only spoke Malayalam but also spoke the language with such a thick accent that it was barely understandable to anyone from outside. Why does Bangalore not own its native tongue then?

My own experience bolstered this argument. I live in Ulsoor, a Tamil-dominated area. It is the place where Karunanidhi ceremoniously unveiled the statue of the Tamil poet, Tiruvalluvar, in 2009. In exchange, the statue of the Kannada poet, Sarvajna, was unveiled by Yediyurappa in Chennai's Ayanavaram. Living in Ulsoor was like living in mini-Chennai. For years, I didn't have to learn Kannada because everyone on the streets spoke Tamil.

But something changed in 2010. I decided that I wanted to learn Kannada. Tamilians joked that the language was very easy to learn (not true). 'You just put the "ha" sound where there is a "pa" sound in Tamil,' said my uncle in Chennai and laughed uproariously at his own joke.

'The script is like a jalebi. Why are you bothering?' asked my aunt.

This attitude typifies the linguistic jingoism rampant in a diverse country like India. We are each so rooted in our mother tongue that it becomes easy to disparage other languages.

I decided to learn the language for the same reason that most people do things that they have long thought about, whether it is pursuing fitness or changing jobs. A confluence of factors came together and made it easy for me to learn the language. I found a tutor; I found people who I could converse in Kannada with; and I found an app that helped me learn Kannada.

The benefits that I have reaped after I forced myself to learn this language have been immense. One of them is that I am able to develop an instant rapport with every person I interact with, ranging from the plumber to the policeman. Although they guess that I am not a Kannadiga because my Kannada is not as fluent as my mother tongue, Tamil, they appreciate that I make the effort. There are two reasons to learn any language—to connect with the people and to connect with the land. This happened to me after I learned Kannada. Suddenly, I understood its movies, music, milieu and multiculturalism.

Are Kannada people jingoistic about their language? Depends on who you ask. Go on a state transport bus and you will hear the Kannada people curse the fact that people from other states have come and taken their jobs. Worse than that, they don't learn the language. Go to interior Karnataka and you will see Kannadigas who are a far cry from the polite people that you associate with Bangalore. In the heartland, people speak in the rough-and-tough fashion that reeks of jingoism. And why not?

As far as they are concerned, their language is better than other languages; their state, food and lifestyle is better than everyone else's. This attitude is no different from the one that some people have in other states.

Linguistic jingoism only happened after the states were reorganized on the basis of language. Before that, the borders were much more porous. Take Karnataka, for instance. Historically, this region was a linguistic salad bowl.

The second oldest mention of the city's name is visible in a Someshwara temple in Madivala, dating back to 1248 CE. Guess the language of these inscriptions—Tamil. The script calls the city 'Vengalur'. The third mention of the city's name is in Kannada literature in around 1300 CE. The fifth is in—again, surprise, surprise—Telugu literature of the 1400s. 'Bangalore has always been multilingual and multicultural,' says Udaya Kumar P.L., when I interviewed him. 'Natively, people speak three or four languages at home. The father may speak Tamil, the mother, Marathi and the aunts, Telugu. They all speak Kannada but they also speak other languages fluently. And this is not recent. This has been the case for centuries.'

Maybe what the outsiders view as linguistic tolerance is really the linguistic adeptness displayed by the people of Karnataka for centuries. Maybe this is the reason why Bangalore has prospered. Multilingual people are mentally and emotionally nimble. They adapt and change as they speak different tongues. They are open to new ideas because each language exposes them to diverse concepts. All of this helps the average Bangalorean embrace new ideas, businesses and cultures. It helps them, in other words, to prosper.

So learn Kannada, not just because you live in Bangalore but also because it will open up this state for you in ways that you cannot even imagine.

What Makes Bangalore 'Home' for Me

My first encounter with Bangalore happened in the 1980s when I was still a student. I would often visit my cousins in Rajajinagar. At that time, Bangalore seemed like a small town with good weather, lovely people, greenery and all the clichés. All those things that old-timers in the city hark back to are true.

I moved to the city in 2005. Even then, the city seemed livable. My children began their schooling here. I think drastic changes started happening when the construction of the metro began, though it was a necessary step.

I find there are many Bangalores in this great city. As an author, the Bangalore that interests me is that of the vendors who walk the street. In Malleshwaram, you'll find baskets of litchis and *jamuns* (black plum) to be sold on the streets. The pyramids of these fruits are beautiful, as are the bundles of *avarekai* (hyacinth beans) and seasonal flowers in the city market. When you walk into Russell Market, you will find exotic vegetables on one side of the street and Indian vegetables on the other. At the Dharmaraja Koil street intersection, there is a woman vendor who knows the benefits of different greens. This is the Bangalore I am interested in; it provides a lot of fodder for anyone who wants to write about it.

And of course, there are the milkmaids and the milkmen. Even yesterday, I saw a man on a bicycle, carrying milk in aluminum pails. They are ubiquitous in my neighbourhood, around Ulsoor. They are part of a way of life that I find hard to replicate in other cities.

The changes I have hoped to see in the city are already happening. Most writers have this element of 'flaneur' where they walk around the streets to get inspired. It is nice to see that public spaces, such as Church Street, are being remodeled for pedestrians. I feel this is still a pedestrian-friendly city, where throngs of people can walk on the streets. I would like this aspect to grow.

I began as a reluctant Bangalorean. Those who grow up in one location all their lives leave a little bit of their hearts behind. I always thought of Chennai as home. But now Bangalore is my home, where I take NRIs out for shopping, go to Avenue Road for street food, to Central Tiffin Room (CTR) or Vidyarthi Bhavan for 'good morning dosas', walk around Ulsoor lake and go birding in Lalbagh or Cubbon Park. The process by which a city becomes 'home' is when every place in it becomes associated with a memory. I have so many associations with the city now. I have spent a lot of afternoons at the tennis association, hanging around while my daughter learned tennis. I have gone rock climbing at the Kanteerava Stadium. I have signed up for 10K runs.

What I regret is not being engaged in the vernacular circles. I haven't been able to do so because I can't read and write in Kannada. On the positive side, there is a community and support for writers (in English) in Bangalore—from lit fests to spaces such as Atta Galatta or initiatives such as The (Great) Indian Poetry Collective. One has the chance to listen to inspiring talks at several venues—from The Bangalore International Centre (BIC) to the National Gallery of Modern Art (NGMA). One can choose to be part of the community of writers; the people here are inclusive, accepting and welcoming.

The fact that I got by for 10 years, communicating in Tamil before I learned Kannada, says something about the city.

20 Things That You Can
Enjoy in Bangalore

'Count your blessings,' Sister Mary would say when I was in high school. I think of her, the stern nun, usually around Christmas. I attempt to do as she ordered. Today's gratitude journals nudge us to do the same thing. Frankly, I find it exhausting to find things every day that I am thankful for. Taking stock once a year is more doable. So, here are 20 things about living in Bangalore that I am grateful for.

1. The flowering trees of Bangalore that bloom season after season in a choreographed sequence, thanks to the German horticulturist, Gustav Krumbiegel. The extravagant blooms include pink bauhinias, yellow tabebuias, white millingtonias, red gulmohar, purple jacaranda, yellow cassias, red spathodea and the fragrant yellow champaka that gives Malleshwaram's Sampige Road its name.

2. The fact that Kannada literature has the second-highest number of Jnanpith awardees, next only to Hindi and more than Bengali or Tamil. They include Girish Karnad, U.R. Ananthamurthy, Chandrashekhara Kambara and a few of the older greats that I refer to below.

3. The famous Indian poet and playwright Kuvempu's book *The House of Kannooru* gives a flavour of the Malenadu that all native Karnataka folks dream about and hanker after. D.R. Bendre, the beloved feisty poet who channelled the soil of Dharwad into his works and often said that the Kannada language manifested itself through his poems. Read

his collection of poetry entitled *Kaamakasthoori* (Musk of Love) to understand the beauty of this language. I cannot read Kannada but I listened to the audio of his poems on a website called *Da Ra Bendre in English*.

4. The genius polymath Shivarama Karanth. One should read his staggeringly prodigious works of fiction, biography, plays and children's books. Another option is to read *Growing Up Karanth*, a memoir written by his children which is an intimate portrayal of the man and his ethos.

5. The musical tradition. Unlike Chennai which is the seat of Carnatic music or Benaras which is one of the foremost '*gharanas*' (lineage) of Hindusani music, Karnataka is home to both Carnatic and Hindustani music. It is truly situated at the cultural crossroads of India. Here, both of India's classical music traditions thrive. Many of the great Indian dance forms, including Odissi, Kathak and Bharatanatyam, flower and blossom in this gracious city.

6. The flora and fauna or the festivals and foods that make up Karnataka. The state's tourism slogan, 'one state, many worlds', does not really do justice. With languid rivers such as the Souparnika, Kaveri and Nethravathi; ancient mountain ranges that include the Sahyadris; and large wildlife reserves such as Nagarahole, Dandeli and Sharavathi, we humans can engage with a staggering array of wildlife in Karnataka, ranging from sloth bears to civet cats and big charismatic mammals such as tigers and elephants.

7. Karnataka's food that is distinct as well as varied. It does not do fusion or dilution, but instead, proudly holds its own. Think of the ragi mudde, for example. These ragi balls need to be dunked in *soppu saaru*—a dal/sambhar-like gravy—and swallowed for them to be a low-carb, slow-release and nutrition-rich food. Think of the variety of brinjals that make up a killer combination in Uttara Karnataka. Stuffed with spices and paired with jowar or jolada rottis, these are to die for.

8. Udupi, the wellspring of the beloved dosas and idlis that are

famous now all over India. Go to Nagarathpete or Avenue Road in Bangalore for small eateries that serve excellent dosas. Go to MTR for *rava* (semolina) idlis, CTR for *benne* (butter) dosas, and Brahmin's Coffee Bar for filter coffee.

9. Thindi Bheedhi or Tiffin Street to taste 'only in Bangalore' delicacies, like Congress buns and a variety of fried beans like avarekai or *kadlekai* (peanuts), both of which are celebrated in Bangalore with *parishes* (pronounced pari-shays), melas or gatherings.

10. The parks. I grew up in Chennai and we had beaches, which inland Bangalore does not have. But what Bangalore does have are parks that act as lungs for the city. Every Sunday, there is a bird and nature walk that is held at Lalbagh and one of the many lakes or *keres* in Bangalore. The details can be found at bngbirds.com. Cubbon Park has a devoted group of runners. Laughter clubs abound. Laugh, walk, run or spot birds through binoculars. Whatever your vibe is, there is a park for you in Bangalore.

11. Vastrabharana, which happens just before the holiday season in early October. It is a time when all the textile-crazy folks of Bangalore make their way to Chitra Kala Parishad (CKP) to buy a year's worth of sarees, stoles and all things textiles. Sisters Mala and Sonia Dhawan broaden the ambit by including all things handmade in the annual exhibitions organized under 'A Hundred Hands', a non-profit trust run by them.

12. The Museum of Art and Photography or MAP, a compact museum that boasts of a fantastic online presence with classes and an encyclopedia of art. The Venkatappa Art Gallery across the street has exhibits that go back centuries. Namu Kini and her art gallery called 'KYNKYNY' champion seasoned as well as new artists. Gallery G is a great central space that puts together interesting talks and exhibits.

13. The BIC, which has become the best place for live talks. If you are flying into town for a day, just pop in to get a taste of what the intellectuals of Bangalore are thinking about.

14. The many craft breweries that have come up all over Bangalore. If fun and dance is your scene, then go dancing or drinking at one of them. Everyone has their favourites. Mine happens to be down the road from me—the 7Rivers Brewing Co. at Taj M.G. Road.

15. Farmlore, arguably South India's best independent restaurant. Drinking and dining clubs love it. There are two wine clubs in Bangalore—the Bangalore Wine Club (BWC) and The Wine Connoisseurs (TWC). One of India's oldest vineyards, Grovers, has its home in Bangalore, as do two of India's best malts—Amrut and Paul John.

16. The Kannada film industry, which is alive and thriving, with films like *KGF* and *Kantara*. The industry is somewhat misogynistic, portraying women in obviously degrading ways; but in this regard, it is no different from the film industries of other southern states.

17. Live theatre, which holds its own in Bangalore, thanks to large spaces like Rangashankara and Jagriti or even small neighbourhood theatres. Malleshwaram's Seva Sadan hosts music and dance performances, as does Basavanagudi's Gayana Samaja. Gokhale Institute of Public Affairs (GIPA) holds talks in Sanskrit, and here too, Bangalore has a coterie of folks who learn and teach this ancient language.

18. Techies and because of them cutting-edge trends, including NFTs (Non-Fungible Tokens) and gaming that have made their way into Bangalore before other cities. The same applies to manga, comics, or for that matter, slam-poetry and stand-up comedy.

19. Beloved bookstores like Blossom, Gangarams and Atta Galatta that are not relics but are lively, much-frequented spaces in Bangalore.

20. The weather. Bangalore has the best weather in Asia. Gentle, temperate and lightly cool, it is a great place to live.

What are your Bangalore blessings?

How Do You Make Friends
in a New City?

Say you move to a new city. Say you move to Bangalore. Beyond *roti, kapda aur makaan* (food, clothes and house), most of us long for a community of friends, especially in the post-Covid world. The problem is that friendships don't materialize out of thin air. They have to be created, connected with and nurtured. The skill of making friends, call it what you wish to, is my favourite answer to an oft-asked question: what do you wish you had known when you were 18?

To that question, I would say: learn to make and keep a large and loose set of friends. British anthropologist Robin Dunbar proposed that the average human can maintain 150 social relationships. This 'Dunbar's number', as it came to be called, became a talking point in many fields—business, team-building, psychology and more. Social networking sites reported that candidates who had 157 relationships reported the highest level of job-offer success.[6] This makes sense. If you are between jobs, the first thing you are going to do is reach out to your friends, or at least, to the people you know, for opportunities. Wouldn't it make sense to have more 'contacts' in that case?

Let me be clear: I am not speaking here of Twitter followers or LinkedIn connections. When I say 'social relationships', I mean relationships created off social media. I am referring to the people

---

[6]Buettner, Ricardo, 'Getting a Job Via Career-Oriented Social Networking Markets', *Electronic Markets*, Vol. 27, 2017, pp. 371–85, https://tinyurl.com/3vscenad. Accessed on 30 April 2023.

you have met at least once in person and people you have kept in touch with. In business, this is known as a 'network', and its verb is 'networking'.

If you are authentic and empathetic, the problem is that networking has such a *matlabi* (calculating), transactional context. It feels opportunistic to cultivate relationships with people just so you can milk them for career opportunities or client contacts. Most of us have trouble doing this.

The solution, at least in my book, is to have a loose set of friends, not because you want to 'network' with them or get something from them but because you share a common interest— be it golfing, playing bridge, trekking or drinking wine.

In my own life, I have found that the best career opportunities came not through diligent networking but from a person who was in the outer ring of the people that I know—the 'loose friendship'. I have watched people who are master 'networkers' and every single one of them hates being called that term. All of them have a few things in common. First of all, they take pleasure in helping people. When they meet a new person, they think, 'what can I offer this person?' rather than 'what can I get from this person?' They do this authentically because they have what books call an 'abundance mindset'. Somehow, they have geared their minds into thinking that what belongs to them will come to them; that the Universe is kind and is looking out for them; that they don't have to scramble or compete for opportunities because the pie is large enough for everyone to eat from. They get ahead, not by taking but by giving. These are not simply good Samaritans, although some of them may be. These are hard-working professionals who think differently.

The next thing that these folks have in common is that they maintain a loose connection with a large number of people—usually, Dunbar's 150 but often much more. They may not speak to all 150 of their connections regularly but they somehow connect on a fairly regular basis, whether it is calling once a year on Christmas or Diwali, sending a birthday card or sharing an article that would be of interest to the other person. The takeaway: they focus on the other person, not on themselves.

The third thing that these master networkers have in common is that they have figured out a way to be part of communities. To me, this is the easiest way to maintain lots of connections.

Bangalore has a lot of such communities, all of which are great if you are new to this city. I'll tell you the ones that I have encountered. Golf is huge here. If you like the game, your network is made. Play once a week, either at the Bangalore Golf Club or Karnataka Golf Association, like my friend Jayashankar does. You will soon have a group of friends that will help you sort through information, share recommendations and help you enjoy life.

I own a Royal Enfield but I am not a motorbike rider. I wish I was because there are a lot of thriving motorcycle clubs in Bangalore. Some ride only Harley, others swear by Enfield. They ride to Nandi Hills on weekends, have a meal there and return. Over several weekends, friendships are made.

I have mentioned the food and wine clubs in the city several times in this book. I have also written about the birding groups. I am an occasional hiker/trekker but not a regular one. Trekking is a great way to meet new folks and keep friendships alive because you are together in nature for at least a few hours. That kind of environment allows one to develop conversation and connection.

So, get out there! Bike, trek, share a meal or play golf or bridge. Make friends; at the end of the day, that's what makes a city home.

FOOD

The Best Restaurants in Bangalore

Known for its tech firms, this cosmopolitan city with a terrific climate boasts of a buzzing restaurant scene. While Covid shuttered many independent fine-dining restaurants, delicious food, both Indian and global, abounds. Here are Bangalore's favourites—some modest but iconic restaurants and some that fit the fine-dining category.

- **Farmlore:** Surrounded by 37 acres of farmland, this serene jewel box of a restaurant seats 16 and is helmed by three chefs, each of whom staged (to use restaurant jargon) at Michelin-starred restaurants in Malaysia, Denmark and Sweden. There is no menu. Instead, what is available on the farm largely dictates what's on the five-course lunch and ten-course dinner degustation menus. Painstakingly sourced native ingredients— Hallikar cow milk, Bannur lamb, Mangaluru prawns, moringa greens, Teja chilies, and Sanikatta salt—make their entrances and exits in the choreographed service. You need to call in advance about wine choices.
- **Karavalli:** Since 1990, Chef Naren Thimmaiah has been serving delicately spiced coastal Indian cuisine to grandmothers, brides, lovers and colleagues. Bangaloreans love his rooted, authentic food—tiger prawn roast, peppery crabs, chicken in a coconut milk stew, as well as unusual and robust vegetables, greens and yams sourced from hamlets by the Arabian Sea. No experiments, no fusion. Just old family recipes that are consistently well-prepared. The restaurant's opening chef, Sriram Aylur, is now at Quilon, London and

you can still taste Karavalli's coastal flavours in his food there.

- **MTR or Mavalli Tiffin Room:** Open since 1924, this unfussy modest restaurant opened its first branch in London this February to much fanfare from homesick South Indians. During the Second World War, when rice was in shortage, MTR invented the rava idli—a steamed dumpling made with semolina and garnished with roasted cashews. It remains a signature offering, along with the crisp dosa-crepes and thali lunches. For many, MTR is a daily habit. A walk in nearby Lalbagh is followed by coffee and vada at MTR. Try this place for breakfast.

- **Falak:** This restaurant—which means 'sky' in Urdu—pays homage to slow-cooked Nawabi food that is borrowed from Greece, Persia and Arabia. Braised and marinated lamb, melting meats, tandoori chicken, slow-cooked dals and copper-pot biryanis are the stars. Chef Farman Ali, 70, the grand old man of Indian cuisine, was lured back from retirement to helm the kitchen and share his secrets. Bangalore-based Grover Vineyards also created a custom Falak blend to go with the white-glove service. Falak wants to be the best Indian restaurant in the continent.

- **Araku Café:** Most Bangaloreans enter Araku Café for its Café L'Orange and its ethically sourced beans grown by tribal farmers in neighbouring Andhra Pradesh. They stay for Chef Rahul Sharma's food. Sharma staged at Noma, which has been listed as the world's best restaurant—twice. Now, he creates stylish small plates to match the minimal white interiors. The excellent produce and dairy come from a local organic farm. The menu roams the world and includes gluten-free and vegan options, including masa pancakes, udon noodles, piquant salads and excellent breads.

- **Kebabs & Kurries:** Within India, ITC restaurants are known for their food. This restaurant in the brand's flagship LEED zero-carbon certified Bangalore property serves terrific North Indian food. Some of the recipes have been taken from their popular Bukhara and Dum Pukht restaurants—the Bukhara dal which is simmered overnight is a must-try, as are the minced lamb kebabs, the smoked chicken and the marinated jumbo prawns. While the brand highlights its sustainably sourced food, what keeps diners returning is the taste which hits the Indian palate spot-on.

- **Far & East:** Beautifully served dim sum and sushi in a sumptuous setting make this a favourite 'date night' restaurant. Chef Atsushi Yonaha, a licensed *fugu* chef sends out high-quality sashimi and *nigiri* with a playful touch. Chef Sean Wong mixes his Malaysian roots with his global sensibility in the wok-fried noodles, Peking duck and dim sums. The service is impeccable. Even those without a sweet tooth will love the desserts, particularly the chocolate pear and yuzu cheesecake. Begin the meal with gin cocktails at Copitas next door.
- **Rim Naam:** Chef Tam stays in the background but her fresh aromatic food sings. Grilled pork rib, thick *tom yam* soup and possibly the city's best *som tam* or green papaya salad from the Chef's native Isan province are some great options to try. Groups opt for shared platters that represent Bangkok, Chiang Mai or Pattaya. The al fresco setting surrounded by leafy trees brings diners to this Central Bangalore spot. The famed Oberoi service doesn't hurt either.
- **Ssaffron:** Since it opened seven years ago, this restaurant consistently gets the highest ratings on crowd-sourced Zomato. Once you taste the mustard salmon tikka and the grilled kebabs, you understand why. With a panoramic view of Bangalore, Ssaffron, despite its unfortunate spelling, exudes warmth and bonhomie. Most diners end up at Hype, the buzzing bar next door, pre- or post-dinner.
- **Windmills Craftworks:** Microbreweries abound in Bangalore. This one was among the earliest to have live music. Comfort food—burgers, pork ribs, interesting salads and grilled meats—is served in a communal setting. The beers keep

changing; a recent hit was their Chai Brown Ale. Live bands perform here regularly, delighting rock-music fans, who drive across town to listen.

The thing with lists is that they have to be constantly updated. For that reason, I have only chosen long-standing restaurants. That said, some restaurants stand out for their longevity and quality. Olive Beach and Sunnys are old favourites and Taaza Thindi in South Bangalore serves one of the best breakfasts in Bangalore.

So how do you find good restaurants? As with anything, you start with your neighbourhood. Find the good ones there by word of mouth and then expand your reach.

Which Breakfast is Better: The Kannada or Tamil One?

In Karnataka, breakfast is a duet; in Tamil Nadu, it is an orchestra.

I may be wading into the Kaveri here, but a question arose recently in my friend group about whether Karnataka's or Tamil Nadu's interpretation of the classic idli-dosa breakfast was better.

Naturally, the Kannadigas thought that the Tamil sambhar was the pits. It lacked jaggery which gave sambhar that sweet-sour flavour that Kannadigas love and Tamilians hate.

The Tamilians thought that Kannadigas do not know how to serve idli or dosa. 'Where are the tri-coloured chutneys?', demanded one Tamilian. 'And why is the sambhar runny?'

As far as vadas go, both parties agreed that Karnataka had cracked the classic *medhu vada* or *uddin vada*, as it is called here. In Tamil Nadu you get tired, soggy and sodden vadas, unless you do some due diligence and choose the right hotel. In Karnataka, and specifically in Bangalore, it is hard to find a bad vada.

The real question had to do with idlis and dosas. Which do you prefer—the Chennai or the Bangalore version? But first, let me lay out the rules of this particular battle. It is only based on tiny tiffin restaurants—called 'darshinis' in Bangalore. Your mother's idli or dosa may be the best in the world but we may not have access to that. We, however, do have access to idlis from Veena Stores, Murugan Idli and Brahmin's Coffee Bar. The question is: which side of the state border makes a better idli and dosa?

Some part of the magic is in the batter. Do you use the 1:4

proportion of *urad* dal to rice or the 1:3? But this, I find, varies within families, let alone across states.

The difference, I think, is how a Kannadiga thinks of an idli versus how a Tamilian thinks of one. For a Kannadiga, the idli and chutney are both soloists playing a duet with each other. Bangaloreans obsess over the quality of the white chutney that is served in most darshinis. Some go to restaurants just for the chutney. Variety is not what they seek. They want quality in that one item. The idlis are equally important in that they need to be fluffy and should spring up when you poke them with your finger.

A Tamilian, on the other hand, thinks of an idli as an orchestra. You need at least three types of chutney—beginning with the white chutney, then some hot or *kara* red chutney made with tomatoes and onions, then a green chutney made with *pudina* or mint, or maybe *kothamalli* or coriander leaves. Three chutneys of three different colours to complement the white idlis. Then, a Tamilian will want some *milagai podi* or idli powder. Finally, most Tamilians want a non-jaggery sambhar that has enough girth for their idli to float in. As for the idlis, they need to be as white and tender as a jasmine flower.

Why are Kannadigas not interested in multiple chutneys? One theory is that Udupi Brahmins, who invented the masala dosa to hide the onions that they wanted to eat, had the same restrictions when it came to chutney. They couldn't do a red chutney because it contained onion.

The Tamil chutney was not similarly constrained. You could add ginger and garlic to the chutney if you felt like it, and, indeed, a ginger chutney makes a fine addition to the Tamil idli platter. Hence, the Kannada idli did a duet with the white chutney; whereas the Tamil idli was the centrepiece of a chutney-laden orchestra.

The difference is just as stark when it comes to dosas. A Bangalorean wants a specific type of dosa, made popular by MTR, Maiyas, Vidyarthi Bhavan and CTR among others. This dosa has to be thick, crispy on the outside and soft on the inside. The batter is less fermented relative to Tamil dosas, maybe because the weather is cooler in Bangalore. The batter has some *avalakki* or beaten rice in it, and perhaps a touch of jaggery which makes the dosa look caramelized and almost black in colour.

This kind of a dosa is an anathema to a Tamilian. In fact, I would go so far as to say that a Tamilian dosa is the opposite of a Kannadiga dosa. Tamilians want a golden brown dosa that is long and thin. It should be crispy outside, but because it isn't as thick, this dosa will also crumple like a sigh after a few minutes on the plate. It will not hold its shape like a thick Kannadiga dosa. Tamilians cannot handle the level of ghee and oil that is poured on dosas in Karnataka.

What about the other ingredients of a South Indian breakfast? The Tamil *upma* versus the Kannada *khara bhaath*. No question. The latter is better. The vada, too, is better here in Karnataka. The *pongal*, though, is better in Tamil Nadu in my opinion. It is thicker. And for those people who think that Tamilian dishes are just over-the-top with too many chutneys and sambhars, I give you the pongal. This herb-infused rice dish is often served with just one accompaniment—a brinjal *gotsu* or a white chutney. A well-made pongal, my brother says, must be eaten in reverential silence.

Karnataka has many more breakfast options relative to Tamil Nadu—and this is perhaps why they lag in the 'number of chutneys' area. At home in Karnataka, people eat akki roti, ragi mudde, avalakki or *neer dosa* for breakfast. Why, then, would you invent so many chutneys to go with your dosa, when you aren't even eating dosas for breakfast at home?

The only thing left is the filter coffee. Where is it better—in Tamil Nadu or Karnataka? Here, both places are even in my opinion; although Bangalore's coffee is a tad bit better because most of the coffee estates are just a few hours away.

So, which state does breakfast better? Karnataka or Tamil Nadu? Your call.

Why Do Bangaloreans Like Single-Colour Chutneys?

For a transplanted Tamilian like me, the most confusing thing about the way Kannadigas eat has to do with chutneys. Why do they have only one-colour chutney and that too, only the white-coloured chutney, which, in my opinion, is the least interesting of them all?

When I asked my friend Ulhas, he looked at me witheringly. To him, the truth was self-evident. 'A Mysore masala dosey already has the red chutney smeared inside. Why pollute it with more chutneys? A simple white chutney will do.'

The thought arose: are Kannadigas minimalists like the Japanese? For years, my theory has been that the only Indian state with a Japanese minimalist sensibility is Kerala—look at their simple khadi-beige *kasavu* attire and their minimally decorated *tharavad* ancestral homes. But in the matter of food, it is the Kannadigas who seem to have adopted a 'less is more' minimalist attitude. One white chutney 'is enough', many Kannadigas will say. But when has just one item been 'enough' in Indian cuisine? More is more till you are stuffed to bursting point. A thali is about choice and abundance—not about 'enough.'

To verify my theory about Kannada food minimalism, I crashed weddings in Basavanagudi, Chamrajpet, Jayanagar and Malleshwaram. These four neighbourhoods, to my mind, represent what we call *'pyoor'* Bangalore, untainted by the immigrants that flock to the Cantonment side and newer neighbourhoods like Koramangala.

In fact, when I moved to Bangalore nearly 20 years ago, I wanted to live in Basavanagudi. We tried really hard to find a place there but discovered that it was hard to dislodge the folks who were already living there. Nobody wanted to sell to us heathens.

What I discovered after crashing many Kannada weddings will seem obvious to anyone who knows the incredible diversity of every state in India. There is no such thing as Karnataka food. What you eat at a wedding will depend on whether the family is Vokkaliga (Gowdas), Lingayat, Kuruba, Bunt, Banjara or Brahmin, not to mention the religious diversity of this state. And the distinctions aren't obvious or correlated. Kurubas are pastoralist cowherds but they also founded the Vijayanagara empire through a long lineage linked to Yadavas. Lingayat literature praises militancy but its followers are strict vegetarians.

Within this diversity, lie some generalizations. All Kannadiga weddings are measured by the quality of their rasam, or saaru as it is called here (this is a piquant soup-like liquid that gets its taste from tomatoes, tamarind and powdered spices). It doesn't matter whether the dozen sweets are well made, although that is desirable. If the rasam (or *rasa* as they call it here) falls short, people will walk out of the wedding feast. The other factor that I noticed was the amount of *kosambaris*, that are poorly described as salads. The third is an obsession with the brinjal, which is prepared in multiple spicy ways. Within this spectrum is the attitude that I am trying to identify. Yes, the true-blue Kannadiga likes variety, but give him good rasam-rice and he is satisfied. Yes, the true-blue Kannadiga likes choice, but give her ragi mudde with *bas saaru* and that is all she needs. Maybe minimalism is the wrong term. Maybe what the Kannadiga cook has mastered is restraint and a keen sense of what goes with which item.

Here are some combinations with descriptions. Notice the lack of multiple items and the specific prescribed combinations.

- **Rava idli with *neer palya*:** MTR invented this idli, made it famous and serves a terrific version of it. You eat it with what

is called a neer palya. 'Neer' means water and 'palya' refers
to a combination of vegetables—much like the Hindi *sabzi*
or the Malayali *thoran* or the Tamil *poriyal*. As a non-native,
this is a non-intuitive combination for me. Indeed, I question
if it is a good combination. But there it is.

- **Maddur vada with white chutney:** To me, the Maddur vada,
invented in a town called Maddur, is arguably the best version
of a vada. It is thin, crisp and filled with spicy goodness like
onions and peanuts. Again, I question whether it needs a
chutney. It tastes pretty wonderful by itself.

- *Nuchinunde* **with** *majjige huli*: 'Nuchi' means broken grains
and most often, refers to broken rice. 'Unde' means round.
'Majjige' is buttermilk. 'Huli' means sour. Majjige huli refers
to sour buttermilk or what North Indians called *kadhi*.
Nuchinunde are oval balls made in the tradition of the
Marathi *modak* or the Tamil *kozhakattai*. They are steamed
dumplings made with grains and lentils. These can be served
with a chutney but Kannadigas also enjoy these with a sour
buttermilk preparation like the kadhi, or a *tambli*. This makes
sense to me because when you eat a few of these balls, you
get very thirsty. The buttermilk assuages your thirst.

- *Guntpongalu* **or** *Paddu* **(shallow-fried balls with fresh
spices) with peanut chutney:** This dish is the Tamil *kuzhi
paniyaram*. Called by many names, it is served with different
chutneys in different regions. I don't like the pinkish peanut
chutney that this dish is often paired with but I do like
the equally pinkish *shunti* or ginger chutney that also goes
with this.

What do these combinations prove? Well, it is clear that Kannadigas
love their food and their combinations. They like variety, but
paradoxically, they also love to have specific things with specific
dishes.

What is your favourite combination?

Is the Kannadiga Sambhar Overrated?

'Tamil Nadu restaurants make lousy sambhar,' said my friend Sree. 'In Udupi and other parts of Karnataka, the ingredients for the sambhar powder are first roasted before being ground; in Tamil Nadu, and to some extent, in Kerala, the ingredients are ground raw. Also fenugreek is either not added or is too little. Plus, tamarind is also too little in quantity.'

'Kannadigas don't know how to make sambhar,' said my relative in Chennai. 'They ruin it by adding jaggery.'

Which version is correct? Well, that depends.

A woman named Geetha M. (who I met on LinkedIn), told me that they don't use jaggery. 'I am a true-blue Mysoorean and even my granny never used jaggery in sambhar. For people with sweet tooths, we used to serve molasses (thick liquid jaggery) with everything. My granny could never eat rice without that. But that's added on separately and provided in a small feeder type of vessel.'

But if you ask the average Kannadiga, they will swear by the jaggery in their sambhar. Makes it tastes better, they will say. And give reasons for it. One man wrote to me saying that it had to do with geography. 'Mean sea level is the difference,' he said. 'Chennai is at zero or say two metres above sea level. Bangalore is about 900 metres. Jaggery in sambhar is probably as much needed due to slow fermentation rate of idli batter.'

What does jaggery in sambhar have to do with idli-fermentation, I don't know. But, at least, it points to the presence of jaggery in this spicy gravy.

If you accept that Karnataka puts jaggery in their sambhar, then the question arises: do you like it?

I dislike the Kannadiga sambhar with jaggery but that is because I grew up in Chennai where mixing sweet things with sambhar is frowned upon. Once you grow up that way, you are doomed because you cannot appreciate the sweet–sour combinations that mark Gujarati cuisine or for that matter, certain specific dishes in all cuisines. I abhor pineapple *gojju*, pineapple pizza and pineapple rasam. To me, this combination dilutes the taste of either and enhances neither. I also dislike mango *morkozhambu* that is made in Palakkad where sweet-and-sour mangoes are added to the buttermilk gravy. For all these reasons, I stay away from sambhar in all Bangalore restaurants. Give me the Thanjavur, Madurai and Kumbakonam sambhar any day. Chennai restaurants, too, make decent sambhar.

That said, I can appreciate the Kannadiga sentiment with respect to how sambhar is used in Tamil Nadu. As one Kannadiga said, 'Sambhar is eaten with rice and is not a good combination with dosey[7]. In Tamilian style, sambhar, chutneys and podi, etc. are all dumped on an idli or dosai. You cannot distinguish one taste from another. In Karnataka, dosey and idli with chutney is the authentic combination. No sambhar needed or added.'

Most restaurants in Bangalore do not serve sambhar with the dosey. Thank God, I say, because I think the Kannadiga sambhar is overrated. A spirited Tamilian who emailed me suggested that this has to do with history. 'Tamizh is the oldest language, second to Hebrew, which obviously confirms that the Tamizh dynasty ruled and reigned [over] India even before India became colonized with the Aryans and those Indo–Babylonian people who settled up north. Why did I give you a short history class? To tell you that it's obvious who took inspiration from the original

---

[7]What North Indians coarsely call 'dosa' is called 'dosha' in Malayalam, 'dosai' in Tamil and 'dosey' in Kannada.

and then modified it into something ridiculous and obnoxious and has the audacity to even make a comparison and take digs at the original. What a travesty!'

The 'original' that he is referring to is Tamil Nadu, with all its dishes, chutneys and sambhars.

The problem in Bangalore is that it is not just chutney or sambhar that the diner has to contend with. Most restaurants add neer palya to certain dishes or offer a *sagu* which is more like a korma with others. Such things have no place in a breakfast meal. These heavy dishes ought to be reserved for later in the day.

There are certain other dishes that are overrated in my view, even though my Kannadiga friends seem to love them. I will name a few.

Gojju avalakki (beaten rice flakes with tamarind and coconut). It is a dish that is served pretty much by itself. This, like a *bhel puri*, is a combination of tastes, textures and flavours. It is an acquired taste. I haven't acquired it yet.

Khali dosey with chutney. Whenever I go to Mahalakshmi Tiffin Room after a morning of birding, all the true-blue Kannadigas opt for this dish. I will never understand why. This is a hole-filled dosey which has the softness of an idli, and therefore, it manages to be neither. It is like a dosey with an identity complex. But my friends love it. They get a thali that has three of these abominations and rave about how the chutney fills the holes and gives it a better taste. If you need a chutney to fill the gaps in taste, you know you are in trouble.

And, thus, my true colours and palate come out. Give me the Kannadiga vade and idli any day. But when it comes to the accompaniments, I'd rather return to Chennai.

The Kannadiga Obsession with the Khara Bhaath

For the average Bangalorean or Kannadiga, there is a two-dish tango that evokes a symphony in their minds. These two dishes are the khara and *kesari bhaath* combination. Not just that, these two dishes are part of an orchestra that includes different kinds of bhaath—*chow-chow,* tomato, *shevige, ghee bhaath,* and the most famous of them all, the *bisi-bele bhaath.* Why do Kannadiga people like bhaaths so much? What is a bhaath?

Well, a bhaath is a rice dish, although these can also be called *chitranna.* But they are entirely different things. The bhaath has the consistency of thick porridge and you could argue that this is the Kannada comfort food, as much a part of their growing up as chicken soup is for the average American. Chitranna on the other hand is flaky and each rice particle stands out separately. In texture, it veers towards an al dente pasta. The rice should not be overcooked in a chitranna; whereas, in the bhaath, it is cooked to the point of softness. Indeed, it is almost congealed in consistency. A bhaath is like a risotto; but for Kannadigas, the bhaaths are a hundred times better than a risotto.

This is not normal to me. As a child growing up in Chennai, if you asked me what my least favourite breakfast dish was, I would say that it was upma. So, imagine my surprise when I moved to Bangalore and discovered that the Kannada version of the upma was a beloved and sought-after dish, renamed as khara bhaath. People went to darshinis specifically to eat it. I would watch with amazement as the average breakfast-eater would ignore the clarion call of the idli, dosa and vada and opt for what I viewed as 'second-category foods', which included the khara bhaath.

Not only that, they would gaze at this dish with intense concentration as they spooned gooey parcels of it into their mouths. Some did the tango, not physically, but in the food-ordering sense. They would order both the khara (which literally means spicy-hot) and the kesari bhaath, and alternate one spoonful with the other. This, to me, is the genius aspect of this combination. The kesari bhaath is what Marathis call *sheera* and the Tamilians call *rava kesari*. In Karnataka, it is given a special status because most darshinis serve it for breakfast. Imagine going to Saravana Bhavan in Chennai and asking for kesari for breakfast. The waiter will laugh in your face. He may offer *basundi* (a sweet dish made of condensed milk), which, for some reason, makes the cut in Chennai. But the average kesari is viewed with mild scorn in Chennai.

That is not the case in Bangalore. Part of the reason behind bhaath's popularity here is the way this dish is served. Typically, it is full of ghee and packed to the brim of a small bowl or *katori*. Then, in a deft move, the waiter will turn the bowl upside down and thump the contents on a banana leaf. Naturally, this ghee-laden mass slides off and wobbles, glistening and inviting on the green background. A good khara bhaath must wobble when you lift up the plate, or else, don't even bother trying it. And to eat it right, you need to get it with the kesari bhaath, made pretty much with the same main ingredients, i.e., rava or *sooji*, cashew nuts, lots of ghee, except the kesari is sweet instead of salty.

The third part of this tango is the green chutney. For some reason, the Kannadigas specifically prefer the green chutney, made with either coriander or mint or both, over the ubiquitous white chutney. The three items on a banana leaf look like space orbs, waiting for aliens to either exit them or devour them.

Which is the best khara bhaath in Bangalore? I embarked on a mission to find out. It was a lot of hard work because I had to eat this dish in all the eateries I frequented instead of automatically jumping to my go-to order of idli-vada-masala-dosa. But some sacrifices have to be made in the name of research. Finally, I have decided that I like the Brahmin's Coffee Bar version the best. Oh, please, don't talk to me about S.N. Refreshments in J.P. Nagar. Any joint that pollutes the khara bhaath with a vada doesn't recognize the potential or the sacredness of this dish.

The Bangalore Coffee Thindi and Oota Club on Facebook recommend Aithal's Mithra Koota but I find their khara, kesari and chow-chow bhaath to be a bit too congealed for my taste. Their shevige (or what Tamilians called *sevai*) bhaath is good and their kesari bhaath has a nice hint of *laung* or clove but their khara bhaath is not up to the mark.

The bhaath that I dislike having at restaurants is the bisi-bele bhaath. You get this dish everywhere but it is always too runny. A good bisi-bele bhaath (which literally means hot lentil-rice) needs to have the heft to hold all the veggies, cashewnuts and seasonings that a Bangalorean aunty throws into it. And it needs to hold its shape, not run and fill the plate.

But back to the khara bhaath and kesari bhaath combination. Why are Kannadigas obsessed with this dish? Is it because it feels healthy and decadent at the same time? Think about it. The dish has a ton of vegetables like carrots, onions, tomatoes, beans, peas and curry leaves. Remove the vegetables and this dish is called *uppittu*. But pack the veggies and it turns into khara bhaath. To this, the cook adds cashewnuts and a ton of ghee. This is the decadence factor. Now, you tell me: how many dishes can you eat where you have the halo-effect of eating vegetables plus the naughty-effect of eating a chocolate? This khara bhaath and kesari bhaath combo gives you both. You become a saint and a sinner in one go.

No wonder the Bangaloreans are scooping it up!

Better than Bhel Puri: Girmit or Mandakki?

To understand the hold that *girmit* or *churmuri* has on people from Karnataka, you have to understand that it is not just a recipe. It is an ecosystem.

The first time I tasted it was when an autorickshaw driver abandoned me in the middle of the road to go buy this dish. We were driving in Akshayanagar (near Begur Lake), when suddenly the driver spotted a shop and swerved sharply to a stop. He got out of the vehicle, put out one finger and muttered, '*Ondhu nimisha* (one minute),' and made the 'swalpa adjust maadi' face that people use when they need to rush to the toilet. But that's not what he was doing. The driver rushed into a tiny shop named Mirchi Mandakki Mane: Taste of North Karnataka. Not wanting to miss out on any taste, I followed him.

It was 4.00 p.m. and the man behind the counter was mixing what seemed like a bhel puri, except it was customized to every customer's taste. My autorickshaw driver, for instance, was giving instructions to the man behind the counter. 'Add more onions, a little more chili powder, little less *sev*,' and so on.

I have never seen such an exchange happen in a bhel puri place, where the customer basically dictates the quantity of every ingredient. The street vendor will probably upturn the bhel puri on the customer's head. This is what makes *mandakki* special. It is a dish but it is also a connection between people; it is an exchange.

Mandakki literally means 'puffed rice'. It is used in various combinations as a snack all over India. Bengal has the *jhalmuri*,

Maharashtra has its bhel puri, and Karnataka has mandakki, also called churumuri or *khara pori*, and a version of it is called girmit.

The difference between mandakki and girmit is that in a girmit, cooked things are added. Just to make things a bit more confusing, there are various versions of the mandakki called churmuri. The *Nargis mandakki* is dry roasted and usually mixed by hand. The flavour comes from chopped and fried green chilies, garlic, curry leaves, turmeric, salt and a pinch of sugar. It is essentially like the bhel mix version of mandakki. The *oggarane mandakki* is similar. Oggarane is called *vagar* in Gujarati, *tadka* in Hindi and *thalippu* in Tamil. It is the tempering that gives flavour to the mandakki. The dry spicy versions of the mandakki are casually referred to as churmuri.

Churmuri and girmit are famous in Davanagere and Uttara Karnataka but you can find them all over Bangalore. The shop that I visited, for instance, has the following items on its menu—spicy girmit, *hirekai bajji* (ridge gourd fritters), oggarane mandakki (seasoned mandakki), *Davanagere girmit* (spicier than usual because it is from Davanagere), *mandakki usili* (where the puffed rice is cooked like an upma), *menasinakai bajji* (green chilies fritters), Nargis mandakki (a specially seasoned puffed rice) and *belluli mandakki* (garlic puffed rice mixture).

What is the difference between girmit and mandakki? Both have a base of puffed rice or khara pori. But the girmit includes a cooked spicy sweet and sour sauce. To a base of oil, you add seasonings such as curry leaves, chopped green chilies, black mustard and cumin seeds, urad and *channa* dal with a pinch of *hing* (asafoetida). After a minute, you add chopped onion and chopped tomato. After they cook, you add some tamarind juice, a little jaggery and lots of powdered spices—turmeric, red chili powder and salt. The result is a thick gojju or sauce that is added to the puffed rice flakes.

The thing that differentiates girmit and the rest of Karnataka's churmuris is the addition of powdered roasted gram powder or what is called *puttani* powder here. This addition to the gojju makes the girmit quite hearty and spicy.

Then comes the reason for the name, which is that you have to stir all these ingredients with a long spoon in a deep pot. Finally, you add raw and finely chopped onions, tomatoes and coriander leaves. Just before serving, you top the dish with sev and maybe a squeeze of lemon. This girmit is served with fried green chilies, in case the eaters want it to be more spicy. You eat it and your head goes 'gir', hence the name. Basically, your head will explode with the heat; but people in Central and North Karnataka love hot things; the spicier, the better.

In Bangalore, if you want to experience the churmuri or the girmit, you need to go on a picnic, either in Nandi Hills or to any nearby temple on a hill. There, you will find families who sit down for a snack after darshan. The mother or aunt takes out all the ingredients for a girmit. Then watch her mix the ingredients with intuitive customization for every palate in her family. With lightning hands, she measures different proportions for each person. Children get less girmit sauce and a bit more sugar. The adults, too, get varying portions of the raw ingredients. The father, for instance, may not like the smell of raw onions, and therefore, gets none. It is this type of customization that is the hallmark of a good girmit.

Like I said, this snack is not just a dish. It is a connection between a mother and a child. It is an ecosystem of encompassing love.

The Pleasures of
Fried Monsoon Snacks

When the monsoon makes its appearance in Bangalore the oil starts sizzling. South Indian kitchens keep their tryst with their gastronomic destiny, not wholly or in full measure (given the number of people who are on intermittent fasting diets these days) but very substantially.

When it rains, South Indian kitchens start taking out their deep-frying *kadhais* (wok). This is not a rare sight as any South Indian *maami* (aunty) worth her salt will make deep-fried snacks almost everyday. It is a neat trick, performed in most traditional homes. After all, what's a better way to disguise leftovers? You simply serve them with piping hot *happala* or *sandige* (fritters). These white tapioca discs will sit on top, like snow on Mount Everest, hiding all flaws underneath. 'Eat your vegetables before you can get dessert' is a Western admonition or threat. Here, in Bangalore, we tempt our families to eat yesterday's curries by serving a savoury temptation on top.

The monsoon is another matter. Whenever there are heavy rains, we get stuck at home. Naturally, we reach for the much-loved snack that we call *nippattu*. Tamilians call it *thattai*. Andhra folks call this *chekkalu*. I would submit that the nippattu is a lot better than the other regional variations because of some subtle yet strong ingredients—the generous use of sesame seeds, peanuts, roasted gram (puttani or *kadalai chutney*) and curry leaves. All this makes the nippattu easy to store and stay crispy for longer, which after all, is the point of South Indian snacks. In that sense, the nippattu is onomatopoeic. It sounds like it tastes.

The recipe is simple. You gently fry skinned peanuts and grind them along with equal quantities of white sesame seeds, roasted gram, and, if you like, *copra* or dried coconut flakes. Then mix rice flour, sooji rava (for crunch) and maida or refined wheat flour (to bind the dish). Add the spices—hing, chili powder and salt. Then add the roasted peanut mixture. Mix oil and water to knead the mixture into small balls. Pat into small round flat discs about the size of the lid of a jam jar. Deep fry.

Some cooks artfully poke tiny holes with a fork on the nippattu's surface for some design and to keep the crispiness. Others pour hot ghee over the whole mixture before adding water and kneading it into balls. No matter, the taste comes from the sesame and peanut mixture and the satisfactory crunch when you bite into it.

The purpose of a nippattu is to please the palate on a monsoon afternoon. Bangalore's nature community, numbering in the thousands, carry nippattu in their backpacks as they hike up Nandi Hills or Savanadurga. Birdwatchers, who throng to Bangalore's lakes, do the same—they carry the crunchies along with their binoculars. Last week, I stood under my black umbrella feeling the thud of a monsoon shower, training my binoculars on a pond heron that was in brown breeding plumage, while my mouth rhythmically crunched on a homemade nippattu. I felt like the heroine in one of Kalidasa's poems.

Most of the Iyengar bakeries in the city sell decent nippattu. But if you want really good ones, you have to find stores with the name 'condiments' in them. Pavithra Condiments in Basavanagudi, Subbamma Stores or Srinivasa Condiments in Gandhi Bazaar and Malnad Condiments in multiple locations are good places to start. Any store with a name that begins with Uttara Karnataka or North Karnataka is also a good bet.

Traditional Kannadigas strictly eat their nippattu at tea time but this rule is relaxed in the monsoon when the nippattu tin is grabbed anytime it rains. To stand on a Bangalore balcony and watch the red earth and pounding rain is an exercise in relaxation. Two things can enhance this experience—masala chai and a plate of six nipattus. Not more, not less. The first two nipattus are pretty much scarfed down. You don't really taste them because you are dunking them in tea. The next two are really about slowing down and taking in the beautiful early rains or *mungaru male* (also a superhit Kannada movie about a stalker; thus, making something that is weird and scary into something that is acceptable). The last two nippattus are really where this snack sings. By then, you've almost downed your tea. Your stomach is full and you've slowed down. You have enjoyed the beauty of the downpour and can finally focus on this humble snack that was, so far, just a crunchy accompaniment. Now you taste the layers, the flavours and the tiny shots of sesame seeds that get stuck in between your teeth. You can taste the peanuts, the bite of chili and the gentle aroma of fried gram. The nippattu is thus elevated; it is no longer just an afternoon snack but a special rainy day memory.

And that, my friend, is the power of a nippattu.

Why Do Bangaloreans Love North Karnataka Food?

Wherever you go in Bangalore, you will see small restaurants that serve North Karnataka or Uttara Karnataka food, specifically banana leaf lunches. The ingredients are well known—jolada rotti (jowar rotis), *badnekayi palya* (brinjal sabzi), *kadalekai chutney* (groundnut chutney) and curd.

North Karnataka or Uttara Karnataka looms large in the food memory of Bangaloreans. Its green forests, verdant vegetation, delicious foods and gentle people are revered in poetry and prose—in the the books of Kuvempu, in movies and music. Uttara Karnataka food, in particular, fits all the flavour profiles that make Karnataka food special. It is both robust and subtle, incorporating masalas that are doused over meats and vegetables. There is also a variety of salads called kosambari, that is served with meals. There is a dizzying array of pickles, enough to make Andhra Pradesh jealous. Then, there are the powders, condiments and sandige or fritters.

In Bangalore, there are many humble darshinis where you can have the famous jolada rotti with all the aforementioned accompaniments. I recommend Kamat Yatrinivas in Gandhinagar, if you can find parking space there. You go to the top floor around lunch time and are shown to a table without a word. Along come the items, one-by-one, served by men carrying those four-in-one stainless steel vessels, where one handle in the centre carries four containers around it.

At Kamat, they give you two powders—deep brown, made with black sesame seeds, and a reddish one, made with ground peanuts. There is the chutney with groundnuts and coconut. There is some *raita* and also the famous Karnataka kosambari made with yellow *moong* dal, shredded carrot, chopped cucumber, garnished with black mustard seeds, green chilies, and if you like, chopped coriander. There is also a soppu saaru made with greens, along with a dal-type preparation, usually made with sprouted green moong, which is very healthy.

The prime mover of this meal is the famous jolada rotti, made of jowar or sorghum flour. At Kamat, you can peek behind the dining room to see industrial quantities of jolada rotti being prepared by two or three people. One rolls the rotti deftly and the other tosses it over the griddle at lightning speed. The rotti puffs up and is sent off to be served. White in colour and with a low glycemic index, this is a great bread for those with diabetes. Usually, there is a slab of butter that is offered with the jolada rotti.

If jolada rotti is the Gangubai Hangal of Karnataka meals, the accompanying tabla player—Sheshagiri Hangal in Gangubai's case—is the *badnekayi ennegai*. This literally means stuffed brinjal in oil (*enne* means oil). It is a luscious spicy preparation that is vaguely reminiscent of paneer butter masala. There are those who argue that the jolada rotti is not the main player but the side dish. After all, the jolada rotti only transports the delicious stuffed brinjal from leaf to mouth, they say. But these are quibbles. One cannot exist without the other. They are like pita bread and hummus—a symbiotic relationship that sings.

The brinjal that is used in this dish is the *matta gulla*, the tender purple brinjal with white streaks. This is stuffed with a masala and then cooked in a gravy made of ground coconut and a variety of spices. If potatoes define Punjabi cuisine, then the brinjal defines Karnataka cuisine. Kannadigas make a variety of dishes with this vegetable.

The Hubli-Dharwar belt is also famous for its *Dharwar peda* and *Godhi huggi*, in which wholewheat kernels are cooked with jaggery, ghee, milk and garnished with cashewnuts and cardamom. It resembles *kheer* or *payasam* in consistency but tastes very different.

Kodubale: The Snack
That Nobody Has Heard Of

There are some snacks that have a pan-regional jurisdiction, while there are those that are authentically linked to one particular state.

Mention *chivda* and quite a few North Indians from different states will perk up. Mention *chakli* and the same will happen to South Indians. But when I ask, '*Kodubale*, anyone?', the response I get is a 'huh?' or a 'kodu-what?' Which is a shame because this snack, much like Congress peanuts or *avarekalu* mixture, is beloved in Bangalore and all over Karnataka.

'Kodu' refers to an elongated shape. For example, in Kannada, *alasande kodu* refers to long beans or snake beans that we typically make into a sabzi. '*Bale*' means bangle and alludes to the shape of these bangle-like round snacks.

The recipe is pretty much the same as in many South Indian savoury items. Dry roast rice flour, along with a little *chiroti rava* and maida. Separately, grind some chutney kadalai or fried gram. To that, add curry leaves, grated coconut and spices—chili powder, salt to taste and a pinch of hing. Grind the flour and spice mixture together. Finally, add a big spoon of piping hot oil. The oil gives the dish its crispiness, so don't miss this step. Give the whole thing a twirl in the mixie. Then take it out, add water and knead into a roti-like dough. Next comes the shaping of the kodubale. First elongate, then bring the two ends together so it looks like a bangle. Deep fry, naturally. Eat right away or store in a jar and savour it for weeks, i.e. if they last that long.

There are three types of kodubale. The Mysuru style kodubale is the most common and is available all over Bangalore. The Malnad style is made with maida instead of rice flour and is smoother instead of grittier. Then, there is a version that is hard on the outside and soft on the inside. This is the *mosaru kodubale* or the yogurt/curd-based variety. In this version, sour curd is added in addition to water and then the mixture is deep-fried. It comes out like one of those vadas sold in Udupi restaurants all over the country. Except that the kodubale tastes infinitely better. In fact, how these big urad dal vadas took over the country instead of the slimmer mosaru kodubale is a mystery. The only drawback of this version is that since it is made from yogurt or curd, it does not last long. You have to make it and eat it right away.

If you want a compromise between crispy and soft, I recommend the Maddur vada as the opening batsman, followed by the mosaru kodbale, both served with a dollop of white coconut chutney. What is a Maddur vada, you ask?

There was once a man—let us call him Basavanna—who was on his way back to his 'native' (a term used in Bangalore to refer to one's homeland). There was only one thing that Basavanna needed to carry back—something that his relatives wanted—and that was a stack of Maddur vadas. To do that, he had to get to Maddur, a town between Bangalore and Mysuru, on the banks of the river Shimsha—a tributary of the Kaveri.

This town in the rich, fertile Mandya district of Karnataka has now become the 'tender coconut capital' of the world, sending its coconuts far and wide up the Konkan coast. People come here for its temples, its sugarcanes and, of course, to eat its Maddur vadas. In what is typical of the Tamil–Kannada debate, the name of the town is open to interpretation as well. Some say that an inscription in Ugra Narasimha Temple calls this town 'Marudhur'. Others say that *'madduru'* means gunpowder and refers to the town's military past. What the place is known for today, however, are its snacks.

Although you can buy these vadas all along Maddur town,

the place to go if you want a bit of history is Maddur Tiffanys on Bangalore–Mysuru National Highway 275. This family establishment is part of the lore of the snack. One of the owners is a descendent of Ramachandra Budhya, who ran VTR or Vegetarian Tiffin Room inside Maddur railway station. Upon learning that a train was arriving early, Budhya hastily converted the mix for his pakoras into a flattened version that would cook faster and sold it as Maddur vada. This accidental invention, with its happy mix of onions, spices, sooji and maida, turned 100 in 2017.

It is the reason why Basavanna's relatives asked him to bring home four dozen vadas, because you see, these vadas can last for a few days without being put in the fridge.

In Bangalore, I go to Woody's on Commercial Street for my Maddur vada fix. And when I go up North, the snack that I carry for my discerning foodie friends is also the Maddur vada, along with, you know it, the kodubale.

Wonders of the Fermented Foods of Karnataka

How many times have you shelled out ₹300 for a bottle of kombucha and wondered why there was no Indian equivalent? Where are all the gut-friendly, probiotic fermented drinks (and foods) in Indian cuisine?

Of course, India has its own healthy drinks. As with anything in India, every state has its own variations. In Kerala and Tamil Nadu, soaking day-old rice overnight, letting it ferment and then drinking it like porridge the following day with pickles is a common practice. Not only does it taste delicious and refreshing, it also fills you up, without making you feel bloated or heavy.

North Indian *kanji*, too, is a delicious winter drink. Often made from black carrots which sadly are not to be found here in Bangalore, this drink too involves natural fermentation for a few days. Nisha Madhulika's popular YouTube channel has the exact recipe. My version comes from my friends, Kavita Gupta and Raj Himatsingka. It was in Raj's house that I had my first taste of beetroot kanji. Made with sliced beetroots instead of the dark carrots, the kanji is made with yellow mustard seed powder, black salt, hing and pepper, which are mixed with beetroot or carrot. You then pour water and allow it to ferment for three to five days. By then, the water is infused with a beet-red colour and the sour flavour from the fermentation caused by the yellow mustard seeds, which warms you up for the winter.

One of my favourite dishes is called *karindi*. It could give all the fermented foods that have become popular a run for their money. I had it for the first time in the Sirsi district in Uttara Karnataka, one of the most beautiful and verdant places in the state. Cleaved by rivers with poetic names such as the Aghanashini, and framed by the Western Ghats, Sirsi is where new flora and fauna are found. It is where school girls with twinkling eyes use giant colocasia leaves as umbrellas as they walk home from school. Some tender touch-me-nots shrink as you graze past them. In this budding blossoming generous land, medicinal herbs sprout from the ground under the pouring rain.

Modest home cooks make nourishing, simple and healthy dishes. Karindi is one of them. The base of the dish is flaxseeds, called *agase* in this state. High in Omega-3 fatty acids, these seeds are left out to dry in the sun or gently roasted. There are several recipes online for karindi.

The one that I make has equal quantities of the following ingredients—flaxseeds, green chilies and garlic. Grind these three together, along with a teaspoon of salt, fenugreek, cumin and black mustard seeds. In the end, throw in a handful of fresh coriander and curry leaves. The paste will end up being a rich green colour. Empty it into a pickle jar. Separately, cut one cucumber and carrot in small pieces. Fold these diced vegetables into the paste. Add a bit of water so that it becomes like a porridge. Cover the pickle bottle with a piece of cloth and leave out in the sun for five days so that it ferments nicely.

The heat of the green chilies goes down as it ferments. So, depending on your spice tolerance, you can adjust the number and size of the green chilies in the recipe. Remember, the fatter the green chilly, the less hot it is. This fermented karindi, which adds spice and sourness to your regular North Karnataka meals, is now ready to use. You may never look at Korean kimchi again once you try the Karnataka karindi.

Karindi is used a lot by the Veerashaiva community who often eat it with jolada rotti. It is kept outside, on the kitchen shelf, not in the refrigerator; and it is served with everything, including hot rice. If you pour a little ghee or coconut oil over it while serving, it adds to the taste. I store it in an earthen pot and have it everyday with pretty much everything. You can also smear it over bread for a taste that is akin to English mustard but more nuanced. It can fare really well in a panini as well because it has depth from the green paste and crunch from the cucumber and carrots.

Recently, I found a win–win recipe which incorporates two of culinary world's current darlings—millets and fermented foods. The fermented food in this combination is the karindi. The other part of this handshake comes from my neighbouring state of Tamil Nadu.

Go to Madurai in the summer and many homes will begin their day with *samai-arisi-kanji*. Made from cooked little millets, this is a mildly fermented drink. What you do is cook a tablespoon of samai (little millet) and mash once it is soft. Add buttermilk to the mashed millets and stir the mix in a glass till it resembles a porridge. Finally, make a tempering to pour on top. Heat oil in a pan, add black mustard and cumin seeds, a pinch of hing, another of salt and a few curry leaves. You can also add diced garlic, if you want to amp up its immune-boosting properties. Add the tempering to the porridge, stir and leave overnight. The heat of Madurai makes this dish ferment overnight. In Bangalore, particularly in September, when the temperature is cool, the fermentation is gentler. In the morning, drink the little millet kanji and have a teaspoon of the karindi. Your stomach will thank you.

Where Are the Best
Masala Dosas in Bangalore?

In their terrific book *The Udupi Kitchen*, the mother-daughter duo Malati Srinivasan and Geetha Rao say that the masala dosa was invented by the devout Madhvas of Udupi to hide forbidden onions into the folds of the dosa.

Bangalore loves its breakfast of idli-dosa-vada-coffee for sure, but in this city, the masala dosa is not the default choice. This is why we stand in line outside Veena Stores in Malleshwaram for its spongy idlis. We drive across town to Brahmin's Coffee Bar for its vada and khara bhaath. Neither of these places are known for their dosas.

If you had to choose the best masala dosa in town, depending on the locality, a few names come to mind.

Here is an incomplete guide to the foods of Bangalore, anchored by the masala dosa. A plate should cost around ₹40. If it is double that, consider yourself getting fleeced.

- **CTR Shri Sagar in Malleshwaram:** This distinctive restaurant at the corner of a not-so-bustling street—at least for Malleshwaram—routinely tops the list for having the best masala dosa in town. You come here for one thing—the butter dosa or benne masala dosa. Crisp on the outside and soft inside, with just the right amount of masala, it wins on every count.
- **Kolla, Malleshwaram:** While at CTR, walk a few yards down to Kolla where goodies from all over the country are stocked. I go there to buy *veppalai katti* (citron leaf powder)

from Palakkad, Grand Sweets munchies from Chennai and some Andhra pickles. They also pack and ship these foods to homesick relatives abroad.

- **Vidyarthi Bhavan in Gandhi Bazaar:** In my opinion, the legend of Vidyarthi Bhavan in Gandhi Bazaar is grander than the actual products. Everyone wants to go here except those that already have. This is masala dosa as theatre. Waiters carry several plates in a line in their hands. Therein lies the problem. Since they cook several dosas at once on a tawa, sometimes the dosas can turn out to be brown or black. The dosa is nice enough but not as tasty as CTR's version. The chutney is poured with a liberal hand, almost as if it were sambhar. There is no sambhar.
- **Mahalakshmi Tiffin Room, Basavanagudi:** The bird-watchers who throng Lalbagh eschew crowded Vidyarthi Bhavan for this MTR. Most often, they have the 'set dosa', which is a favourite of Bangaloreans. What is a set dosa? It is a plate of three thick round dosas, placed one on top of the other, served with sagu, a kurma-like confection. Try it. The signage here is in Kannada, which signifies its authenticity.
- **Mavalli Tiffin Room:** Don't eat the masala dosa here, I beg you. Instead, try the dish they invented, i.e. the rava idli, which is fantastic.
- **Vasudev Adiga's Paakashala in Ulsoor:** You can get your preferred dosa here but I go to this place for their excellent vadas and tasty chutney.
- **Om Sai Skanda Dosa Camp, Cambridge Layout:** Type in the words 'dosa camp' and you get literally hundreds of dosa outlets all over Bangalore. Depending on location, you can choose one that is close to you and it is likely that you will get a good breakfast. It is hard to mess up a recipe that has been empirically perfected by South Indians. I discovered this one because of the Sai Mandir down the road. You stand outside as there's no seating and eat your dosa along with school kids and worshippers.

- **Sri Krishna Kafe, Koramangala:** Koramangala is bustling with food outlets which kind of sucks if you don't live near Koramangala. This one is great for dosas.
- **SN Refreshments, J.P. Nagar:** If you go to Bannerghatta National Park and you should it is worth stopping at this place en route for its excellent breakfasts. They have soft idlis that even Veena Stores would get a complex about and folded-over masala dosas.
- **Maiya's, Jayanagar:** I like Maiya's because unlike many breakfast outlets, they serve rava dosa, favoured by Tamilians. I end up buying some of their ready-made foods as well.
- **Umesh Refreshments:** Manas Krishnamoorthy, the general manager of ITC Gardenia, told me about this place. In leafy Kumara Park, you stand outside and eat your triangular masala dosa in silence.
- **Beyond the masala dosa:** Like I said, the masala dosa is not the be-all and end-all for us Bangaloreans. To get an idea about the variety of choices available here, visit the Facebook page of the Bangalore Coffee Thindi and Oota Club. It is there that I learned about the *ghee sabakkai* (dill) dosa served at Cottonpet Tiffin Rooms in Basavanagudi, which is where I plan to go next.

I haven't even got to the dosa outlets on Thindi Bheedhi or Food Street in V.V. Puram which deserve their own essay.

What's your favourite dosa place in Bangalore? Surprise me!

Which Are the Best Restaurants for Karnataka Food?

I am not sure that I can show my face in Chennai again, and indeed, I feel bad even saying this, but Karnataka is more diverse in its food than my native Tamil Nadu or Kerala where my ancestors hail from. Part of the reason is the terrain. You have the Konkan coasts and the Sahayadri mountains, thick Western Ghat forests and the flowing Kaveri in Karnataka.

When I moved here about 15 years ago, I used to get confused between Uttara Karnataka and Uttara Kanara. The former is a huge region that includes Kalaburagi, Bidar, Bagalkote and other parts of the Deccan. The latter is a coastal belt that includes Karwar and Malenadu—a hilly region that includes Sirsi, Shivamogga and other districts of the Western Ghats. Most people say North and South Canara district.

If you had to divide the state culinarily, it would be Uttara Karnataka or North Karnataka;, the Mysuru-Mandya district; Konkan or coastal Karnataka which is Mangaluru and upwards on the coast to Karwar; and Coorg. Malenadu is nominally part of the coastal region but deserves a separate mention in my mind, as does Gowda food.

Each of these regions are distinctive. The problem is that unless you go to these places, regional food is hard to come by in Bangalore. Regardless, here are a few region-based restaurant recommendations that you need to try; and some more.

- **Mangaluru food:** Sannadige in Goldfinch Hotel and Kudla in Ramanashree Hotel—these two places were recommended by

Chef Naren Thimmaiah who runs the beloved and acclaimed Karavalli restaurant. All three restaurants specialize in seafood and coconut-rich Mangalorean cuisine flavoured with spices most probably from Kundapur.

- **Gowda food:** Bangalore Oota Company—they focus entirely on food from Karnataka, specifically from the Bunt and Gowda communities that they belong to. What makes Gowda food distinctive, I asked Divya. Here's what she said: 'Coriander in all its forms—fresh and powdered—green chilies rather than the usual red Bydagi chilies that this state loves, mutton and chicken rather than seafood because Gowdas generally live in interior areas like Malenadu and Chikkmagaluru and the hearty ragi mudde (cooked ragi ball), accompanied by soppu saaru or sambhar with greens.' Divya said that swallowing ragi balls, rather than chewing them, is better because chewing releases sugars.

- **Uttara Karnataka food:** Kamat Yatrinivas or Kamat Bugle Rock for a typical lunch of jolada rottis, badnekayi ennegai and a variety of chutneys, all served on a banana leaf. In addition, look for any place that says 'Khanavali' and you can bet that you will get good food there. Imagine my surprise when I walked into MTR 1924 on St Mark's Road and found a new place called The Brahmins Khanavali that served excellent Uttara Karnataka food in the heart of town.

- **Vegetarian food from the Madhva community:** Udupi Sri Krishna Bhavan in Balepet or Basavanagudi serves a good banana leaf lunch with a variety of kosambaris, palyas (or vegetable curries), terrific rasam and other dishes.

- **Coorg food:** Coorg food is hard to come by even though it looms large in the minds of Bangaloreans. Two choices suggested by my Coorg friends are Pig Out, a cute take on the famous pandi-curry or pork curry of Coorg, and The Coorg Food Company in Koramangala. For the culture and flavours of Coorg, read Kaveri Ponnappa's writings.

Other Noteworthy Restaurants

- Oota in Whitefield, is run by three veteran Bangalore hands. 'Oota', which means food, does Karnataka cuisine in a thoughtful expansive way.
- Asha Food Camp, Malleshwaram is where Kannadigas go to eat other stuff. Owned by Madhvas from Udupi (disclosure: the owner lives in my building), has a bit of everything—Chinese, North Indian, South Indian, soups, you name it. The reason people go to this place is the tasty, reasonably priced food.
- Old Bangalore families have some specific haunts that have nothing to do with Karnataka food but have more to do with quality and longevity. The food at Bangalore Club, for instance, is nothing to write home about; Century Club is better. But multigenerational families gather here for the ambience and to meet-and-greet.
- Similarly Royal Afghan or Dakshin at ITC Windsor, or Windsor Manor as Bangaloreans insist on saying, are old favourites. People have been going to these restaurants for decades. Dakshin serves good food from the southern states, but Royal Afghan is straight on Northwest Frontier food. It is terrific food, and my friend and birdwatcher-ecologist, M.B. Krishna's brother, M.B. Prakash, plays the accordion here during dinner. Or at least, he used to.
- Sunnys too is a Bangalore habit. People have been visiting Sunnys for years, following its owner, theatre maestro Arjun Sajnani and his team, from location to location.
- The same with Watsons, a well-priced pub where boys went before they became the men of today. Airlines Hotel and Corner House still draw college kids who have come back home from all parts of the world.

Good restaurants are not just in the business of selling food. They are in the business of selling memories. For some of these restaurants that I've mentioned here, memories are a function of their longevity—we are able to go back to these places time and again. But that isn't enough. The food had better be good, else none of the nostalgia will matter. All the places listed here fit that bill.

What Are Bangalore's Trending Restaurants?

Where do the young and restless go to enjoy food and drink in Bangalore?

Let's face it. A lot of what is considered best is subjective. Even if you go through crowd-polled websites, it is a hit or miss. The other day, I went to Sante Spa Cuisine, awarded 4.8 stars on Zomato. The service was lethargic, the food so-so. Ditto for Manjit da Dhaba near Bangalore East station, which has 4.5 stars on Zomato. You climb up the stairs into a dark no-frills space and get excited. It has the proper dhaba look, you think. *The food must be good.* Well, let's just say that it ain't a patch on Punjabi dhabas. So what's the takeaway? Mine is not to trust Zomato ratings because while they are crowd-polled, they aren't customized or geared to your taste. My technique is to ask trusted friends and then account for their biases. When a Kashmiri friend says the food is too spicy, I automatically think it is probably perfect for spice-loving me.

So what's new and hip in Bangalore? Well, one trend is animal-inspired names—Trippy Goat, Red Rhino, Gawky Goose, Rogue Elephant, Tipsy Bull, Boozy Griffin… Seriously? Is this the formula? Pick a creature, any creature. Then attach an adjective to their name. Open a restaurant. That said, these restaurants are decent. Trippy Goat is owned by Vishal Nagpal, an old Bangalore restaurant hand and a friend. Red Rhino is a popular microbrewery. College kids love Gawky Goose for the live music and the large space. Rogue Elephant is in a terrific location in

Basavanagudi—opposite Krishna Rao park and next door to Ambara where handcrafted goodies await.

The other restaurant trend is misspelling names which drives me nuts. This is particularly true for the many microbreweries in Bangalore. Byg Brewski, Brewklyn Microbrewery, Seven Storyss, Shakesbierre, Ssaffron, Communiti. What in heaven's name are these guys thinking? Is it numerology? Or an attempt to be cool? A bit of both, I think.

Independent restaurants open and close. Abhijit Saha, who introduced molecular gastronomy via his much-feted and now-closed restaurants, Fava and Caperberry, is now a consultant. He has collaborated with two new restaurants, The Pet People Café and Glass Bar and Kitchen.

Koshy's thankfully remains open and people keep going to it. Corner House and Airlines Hotel still draw a crowd to their leafy centre of city location. My brother and I still like Tandoor where we used to take our kids and now he goes there with our Mom. Ebony, which overlooks M.G. Road, suddenly gained clients during Covid because of its open-air views of the city.

Hallowed bakeries like O.G. Variar and Iyengars still hold their own. Albert Bakery on Mosque Road still sells its popular *khova naan* or bread stuffed with khoya. The small red velvet cupcakes with fresh cream from Glen's Bake House are eminently scarfable. Fabelle's by the ITC group, has—and I hate to say this, given that this is a giant five-star chain in the company of Iyengars and Variar bakeries—excellent dark chocolates. Zed the Baker has made Zaid Sait a hit in Bangalore.

Military hotels are going strong. Empire Hotel on Church Street, where the drunk and the depressed show up at 3.00 a.m., still survives. Nagarjuna and Bheema's haven't messed with their Andhra menu, thank God. Eden Park, with its hearty biryanis and strong liquor, is still popular among college kids. Hunan's signature sauces are now delivered to homes, thanks to Covid. People-watching is still possible, even in laidback Bangalore at UB City's many restaurants. The 12th Main Road in Indiranagar is where you need to go for dining choices. Konark is an old haunt that still serves excellent breakfasts. Bangaloreans finally don't have to crib about the terrible paneer here. We each have our neighbourhood place for paneer—I buy mine at Infinitea Café on Cunningham Road which imports Delhi paneer daily.

Microbreweries deserve a separate essay; and Toit has reopened, hallelujah! Arbor Brewing Company attracts a loyal University of Michigan crowd including my husband, who doesn't drink but accompanies me out of solidarity. Geist beer by our friend, Narayan Manepally, is opening new branches. Brik Oven's arugula pizza still rocks. Lavonne's almond croissant competes with Magnolia Bakery's croissants. Honore Bakery's seeded sourdough still comes home every few weeks. Tewari Brothers' dal puri and aloo sabzi are to be savoured in solitude. Anand Sweets and Bharatiya Jalpan on Commercial Street serve excellent chaat—okay, not on the same level as Delhi or Mumbai. Sattvam in Sadashiv Nagar is where ISKCON-loving families go regularly to dine.

So where am I going to go? Well, there are a few places I haven't been to and want to try out. Three Chennai chefs are running Salt and lots of my foodie friends recommend it. Chef Regi Mathew is rocking it at Kappa Chakka Kandhari—the name is authentically vegetarian even though friends love the crab and seafood dishes. Pizza Bakery is on my list too, so I can see if its pizzas are as good as the ones at Sunnys and Brik Oven. Rameswaram Café's ghee podi idlis have created a traffic jam outside, so, of course, I have to check out if it's as good as those at Murugan Idli in Besantnagar, Chennai.

Oh, and I still need to check out a whole lot of microbreweries. Give me a few months for that.

What to Eat When You Are Halfway Vegan?

What do you eat when you want to go half-way vegan? Eat beaten up yogurt mixed with herbs, that's what. It is depressing. Here I remain, perched on the higher end of the weighing scale, basically hating myself for over-eating, over-boozing and falling off my exercise routine. How to detox now? How, now, to stop the steady upwards march of my Body Mass Index? How to stem the not-so-steady ballooning of various body parts?

The answer, I say, is tambli. Never heard of it? Never mind. Tambli is a cross between a chutney, raita and a lassi. It is served in coastal Karnataka, in Mangaluru and upwards, usually before the rasam course of a meal. It is considered cooling during the hot and humid summers.

Tambli or *Thambuli* is made with herbs and curd. It can be of a thickish texture or have a buttermilk consistency. I have made it with the Brahmi leaf which is medicinal. My friends who grew up in Shivamogga district talk about kids being compulsorily given this brahmi-leaf tambli dish in the early years to improve their memory.

The tambli, it seems to be, was born of one impulse—the availability of an abundant quantity of coconut. A favourite tambli in this season veering towards cool days and nights in Bangalore is the *dodda patre tambli*. Called *ajwain patta* in Hindi, *omavalli* or *karpuravalli* in Tamil, this leaf—Indian borage or *Coleus amboinicus*—has a number of health benefits. When you have a cold, a decoction or *kashaya* made of these leaves is great to expel phlegm.

I learned to make this tambli by watching 'Swayam Paaka', a Kannada cooking channel. The cooking method is quite simple. You fry the ajwain leaves in ghee till they reduce in volume and go from bright green to a dull green. Then, you add a handful of grated coconut, salt, half a teaspoon of cumin seeds, some black pepper and grind the whole thing in a grinder. Lastly, you add sour curd or sour yogurt—about half a cup—which waters down the chutney-like mixture. Pour it out and season with a tadka of black mustard seeds and cumin seeds.

In the verdant Malnad or Malenadu areas encompassing the slopes of the Western ghats, they serve this thin yogurt tambli at the beginning of the meal, along with rice to settle the stomach. Some use *amla* (gooseberry) as base, others use tomatoes or greens. A popular one is ginger tambli, made with ginger and one green chili if you prefer this taste to black pepper, all ground together with yogurt. In the summer months, this serves as a refreshing counterpart to piping hot rice. In the winter months, the same dish becomes a digestive.

Which brings us to the key question: is there any other culture that is as obsessed with the yogurt-coconut combo as we South Indians are?

At my high school, it was common to refer to South Indians as 'curd rice' or '*thayir saadam*'. It was a slur only in the manner that most high school nicknames are affectionate insults anyway, and they were dispensed to all categories and classes of students without fear or favour anyway. But in its capture, the epithet is true. Barring Kerala, which prefers buttermilk, the three other South Indian states, especially Tamil Nadu and Karnataka are suckers for a well-made curd-rice. The dish goes by many monikers. The big-daddy of them all is the *bagala bhaath*, served at weddings. This version has ruby-red pomegranate seeds, sliced green chilies roasted in hing that gives it a wonderful flavor; and it is topped with chopped coriander leaves and a tempering of black mustard seeds, urad dal and channa dal. I eat it with a very specific pickle called *vepallai katti* that is a specialty of Palakkad where my ancestors come from. It is my pick-me-up and rescue-remedy after a night on the tiles. As a cure for hangovers, it has few equals in my book.

In Karnataka, the same curd rice is called *mosaru anna*. Kerala takes a different tack and serves you boiled buttermilk or *kachiya mooru,* a watered down chaas-type drink that you can—if you like a weakened version of curd-rice—pour over your rice. This is because Ayurveda takes a dim view of the thick curds that we all prefer.

Karnataka's tambli in my view checks a dizzying array of boxes, some of them contradictory. Thanks to the ground coconut, it has a girth that helps keep the anti-thick curd Ayurveda puritans happy. At the same time, it also satisfies those who like their curd thick. It can be served over hot rice, which also is something Ayurveda advocates—don't eat cold things. Since the tambli can become a colourful chameleon, depending on what you grind with it, it keeps finicky youngsters happy too.

For these and other reasons, I hereby nominate the tambli as my go-to dish for the summer months.

Is Bangalore the Foodie Capital of India?

If you search 'Bangalore foodies' on Facebook, you will find not one or two but a whopping 26 groups. Go ahead. Try it. A similar search on Delhi foodies made six groups turn up, and this includes 'Delhi Noida Food Freaks'. Search Facebook for 'Mumbai foodies' and there are eight groups, even after expanding the ambit to include 'Mumbai Food and Drinks Club'. Kolkata foodies showed seven, including 'Bengali foodies'. 'Chennai foodies' showed 10, including a foodies group that communicates in Tamil.

Does this mean that Bangalore is the foodie capital of India? That it is the one city that takes food seriously to the point of forming communities around it and obsessing over obscure and mundane recipes? I believe so.

In the name of research, I have had to prowl most of the Bangalore foodie groups both online and offline. Some are rabidly commercial, with home cooks and chefs posting recipes, offers, discounts and rewards. Others, such as the Bangalore Biryani Club and the KLG or Koramangala Lunch Group, meet in person at different outlets. Most of my non-vegetarian friends say that the pleasures of biryani are lost on vegetarians like me. So I joined the KLG for lunch at a pizza restaurant. For the last seven years—and that's a long time—except during the darkest days of Covid, this group of about 15 people have met every Wednesday at one o'clock in the afternoon. Founder Nimish Gupta posts the restaurant name where you have to gather on the morning of the meet-up. You show up, eat, drink and share the cost. That's it. They welcome guests. If you are flying into Bangalore on a Wednesday and want to join a group of passionate foodies for lunch, you can find them on Facebook and ask for the location, says Nimish. On the day that I attended, about seven members were in attendance. I asked them for a list of obscure places and their top choices. Here are their recommendations in their words:

- **Street Storyss:** All vegetarian food, ranging from fusion to Jain. Well presented. Modern ambience. (Aarti and Vivek Vaid)
- **Bamey's Nepali Bistro:** Excellent simple food with unusual tastes. Good, even for vegetarians. (Aarti and Vivek Vaid)
- **BYLI (Bet You Like It):** All-day dining. Great breakfast dishes. Eggs, toast, waffles, pancakes. In Kalyan Nagar. (Paul Abraham)
- **7 Plates:** Tight menu. Also in Kalyan Nagar. Go here for the kebabs or the rolls. They are terrific. (Paul Abraham)
- **Naati Sogadu in Hebbal:** You should try their vegetarian biryani and their Hanumanthu pulao that is a version of the famous original Hanumanthu pulao in Mysore. (Devesh Agarwal)
- **Sendhoor Coffee:** They have excellent ghee podi idlis, vadas, paniyarams and multiple varieties of dosas. And, of course, coffee. (Devesh Agarwal)
- **Polamma's Mess:** Go here for wholesome Andhra meals. (Jaideep Gaandhie)
- **Mangamma Tiffin Room:** You should just go here for about 10 varieties of idlis and dosas. (Jaideep Gaandhie)
- **Sri Amba Bhavani Caterers:** You should go here for excellent non-vegetarian food. Mutton and chicken biryani.(Kunal Bysani aka 'Ghatotkacha' on Instagram)
- **Mulbagal dosa:** This is a special dosa made on a thick cast iron tawa, with lots of ghee and oil. Sometimes they fill the dosa, which is crisp outside and soft inside, with lemon rice, chutney, potato palya. A complete meal. (Kunal Bysani)

- **Shetty Lunch Home:** Good authentic Mangaluru food. Ghee roast dosas and lots of lunch options, including a thali. Reasonably priced beer. (Nimish Gupta)
- **Dalma:** Odia food is little known here in Bangalore and Dalma does a great job of presenting it. Unusual ingredients and well-made food. (Nimish Gupta)

Every city has its foodies who will swear by certain cuisines and neighbourhoods. These are some suggestions that all of the KLG members present that day agreed upon, calling these eateries the 'hidden gems' of Bangalore—their top picks, in other words. And I am sure this is a list that will keep on having many additions and revisions.

Sri Krishna Café is an old and favourite establishment. China Pearl is great for...well, the name says it all. And 154 Breakfast Club has a variety of egg-based and non-Indian breakfast dishes. Naati Kafe serves native Bellary chicken, akki-rice rotis and traditional Kannada food. If you crave Singapore-style hawker food, go to Nasi and Mee.

Lastly, let me put in a plug for my secret place. I go to Tewari Brothers fairly regularly, often by myself, for a quick and delicious lunch of their puri-aloo. I order, sit by myself and eat the food quietly.

DRINKS

What Kind of a Coffee
Drinker Are You?

In my mind, there are only two types of coffee drinkers. And there are only two South Indian states that can lay claim to coffee: Karnataka and Tamil Nadu. According to an India Coffee Board publication, South India consumes 78 per cent of the Indian coffee. Among the South, Tamil Nadu accounts for 36 per cent and Karnataka, 31 per cent. Andhra and Kerala are 18 and 15 per cent respectively.[8] The latter two states make better tea than coffee. Between Tamil Nadu and Karnataka, there is the usual divide and endless debate about which coffee is better. The answer is so obvious that I don't even need to mention it here. My question is much more nuanced and connected to those of us who wake up to filter coffee every morning. The question is: where do you buy your coffee from?

Are you a 'coffee works' kind of person? Or are you one of those high-falutin, cold-brew drinking Maverick & Farmer? Bangalore is full of places where the coffee...well, works. There is Sri Suma Coffee Works in Jayanagar, Gokul Coffee Works on Gandhi Bazaar, Sri Vasanth Coffee Works on Sajjan Rao Road, Mahalakshmi Coffee Kendra in Chamarajpet, and Sri Vinayaka Coffee Beans in Malleshwaram where you can drink and feel lovely.

These are honest, homely and heritage coffee purveyors who sell the beans or ground coffee to you without too much fuss

---

[8]'Coffee Consumption in India–2009', *India Coffee Board*, https://tinyurl.com/7ps3hap6. Accessed on 30 April 2023.

about which unpronounceable estate it is from and whether it is plucked without child-labour and whether the beans are unsprayed, organic, fed by cowdung from desi-breeds and harvested in the moonlight by light-fingered women. At the end of the day, all you want is filter coffee beans and not some PhD dissertation, right? The fact that we all morph into versions of ourselves that care about organic foods and child-labour later in the day is another matter. Maybe it is the filter coffee that makes us enlightened beings that suddenly spout homilies about regenerative agriculture and reductivism in art.

To me, good filter coffee bought from a store that has a Western-sounding name is an oxymoron. It is not to be trusted because the brands that proffer everything from cold-brew to pour-over along with 'oh-by-the-way, we also have filter coffee', don't know what they are doing. They try to please everyone and end up pleasing no one. Give me a Panduranga Coffee any day, couriered straight from Chikkamagaluru. Failing that, give me Cothas coffee with 15 per cent chicory.

I love the black baza, a bird found in the Northeast, but please, I don't want it in my coffee. Nor do I want any sleepy owls, flying squirrels or the blue tokai (feathers) of a peacock. I don't want to slay coffee or rage with it or surf the third wave. Araku sounds like *arachu*, which means 'grind' in Tamil. I like *nellikai* or amla but not in my coffee. Please don't preach to me or tell me that it is a Frenchified Cafe L'orange drink, tasty as it is. I just want my coffee served in silence and in glass cups, like at Airlines Hotel.

I like my coffee the way I have always had it. The way my mother gave it to me—sans questions, interrogations and a halo-effect lecture about grind and source. Just give it to me already, why don't you?

And please don't go on about single-blends because we Indians who drink filter coffee already know one inescapable fact: single blends don't work in filter coffee. Blended coffee is the way to go. Medium roast also doesn't work in filter coffee, beloved as it is with the 'aroma police' of the coffee-loving world who express disdain for dark roasts because they kill the smell of the coffee, according to them. But medium roast in coffee means that the decoction won't be dark, which creates a whole assembly-line of problems. If the decoction isn't dark, the coffee will look milky, not dark brown even with a little milk. It won't taste strong because the milk flavour will dominate. Medium roast just does not work for filter coffee.

Single-estate coffee has specific contours and flavour profiles that may suit black coffee but when you pour hot milk on it, the decoction gains an unpleasant edge, like day-old wet laundry. To make good filter coffee, you need the magic ingredient called 'chicory', either 15 or 20 percent, depending on how thick you like your coffee. And you need frothing that comes from two hands, two tumblers and a precise wrist.

My taste in filter coffee is a result of what was served at my home in Chennai. Isn't that true for all of us? And you know what the best part is? Amongst filter coffee drinkers in traditional Chennai or Bangalore, there is consistency of taste. Homes that made good coffee, uniformly served coffee with broadly the same taste profile. You could bank on it. So, once you did the due diligence on which house served good coffee and not a watered-down decoction with day-old milk, you could go back time and again. There were no unpleasant surprises. This is because good filter coffee relies on more than one factor for perfection. You have the decoction which has to be of a certain thickness. Then, the hot frothy milk. And then, just enough sugar to reduce the bitterness without messing with the taste.

Good filter coffee is not about provenance. It is about proportion. Write that on a sign. Hang it around your neck.

So all these people who write about their coffee being grown in such-and-such hills, surrounded by wild elephants, don't know what they are talking about. As for the Kopi luwak beans that are eaten by the Asian palm civet which then excretes these beans, thus making them the most expensive coffee in the world, well, all

I can say is that I have tasted it and it is shit coffee, quite literally.

My father loved coffee beyond logic or reason. Once a month, he used to take me with him to the local Leo Coffee store. No gleaming shelves, no filter press, nor cards describing the elevation of said coffee or the name of estate. Instead, there were gunny sacks full of coffee, a grinder and the aroma that permeated the entire neighborhood. My Dad would choose a blend of plantation, peabury and chicory and have it ground right there. We would carry it back in a bright yellow Leo's coffee bag. Sometimes, we would go to Narasu's coffee for a change. But never to cafés. We didn't trust café coffee at home. That was only for impressing foreign visitors who couldn't pronounce long Indian names.

With that, we come back to the question that is asked often: where do you get better filter coffee—Chennai or Bangalore? The answer is so obvious that I don't need to repeat it here.

How a Pensioner's Paradise
Became a Pub City

god and a goddess came down to earth. They took a nap under a tall tree. When the god woke up, he was thirsty and drank the sap that was flowing down the tree, not realizing that he was drinking toddy from a palmyra palm tree. Soon, he became amorous with his wife, who understood what had happened. In an effort to calm her husband down, she massaged the palm's trunk to make the sap flow back upwards. This gravity-defying feat was possible because she was a goddess. The slumbering god woke up and wanted more *kallu* liquor. Not finding any, he slapped his thigh and created a man out of it. 'Climb this tree and tap the sap,' commanded the god. Thus, toddy tappers were created. They were called Daivas or Thiyyas in Kerala and Idigas or Edigas in Karnataka.

Fun fact: Toddy is tapped from either *Palmyra borassus*, or from *Eecahalu phoenix* and additionally from *Baine careyota* in the ghats and coastal region where it grows.

Lots of Edigas settled in Bangalore. But the man who belonged to arguably the first family of liquor in Bangalore was not part of this community. Vittal Mallya, a Gaud Saraswat Brahmin, founded the United Breweries Group, which you could argue is a forerunner to all the brewpubs dotting Bangalore today. But several other Idigas made their mark in many fields. Filmstar Rajkumar is an Idiga, as is former Chief Minister, Bangarappa. All of them thronged to Bangalore, bringing their trade and skills with them.

They worship Yellamma Thaayi and are more popularly known by a name you might recognize—Gowdaru or Gowdas.

This fanciful legend is perhaps made up but the basic facts about the toddy tapping community hold true. In fact, the Idigas later morphed to managing businesses, and not just in the liquor industry. Sure, they run a lot of the IMFL (Indian-made Foreign Liquor) shops all over the metropolitan region but they also start newspapers—*Prajavani*, the Kannada newspaper, was founded by an Idiga.

Fun fact: Idigas are patriarchal and speak Kannada or Telugu but toddy tappers of the coastal areas are Billavas who speak Kannada or Tulu. They are matriarchal like the Malayalam speaking Tiyas, who live south of Kasargodu. Billavas are Bhoota worshippers.

Combine the Idigas with the British and you have an unbeatable confluence of events and people, which led to Bangalore becoming a breezy Pub City where drinking was easy. Today, Bangalore has a growing number of microbreweries. Two of them—Byg Brewski in Hennur and Windmills Craftworks in Whitefield are in the Top 30 list of Best Bars in India.[9] Windmills has also gone international with an outpost now in Texas. Several of Bangalore's microbreweries are now bringing their beer to retail shelves like Red Rhino and Arbor, with Toit expected to follow suit soon.

So where do Bangalore's 20-year-olds go to drink and dance? This group, coveted by restauranteurs, goes out a lot. While they are generally forgiving of bad food, they instantly change loyalties the minute they sense that the place has lost its edge. Best of all, they go out in herds. So, here are some recommendations.

- **The 13th Floor:** This restaurant and bar is beloved because of its affordable food, great views, well-priced drinks and

---

[9]'India's Top 30 Bars', *30 Best Bars India 2022*, https://tinyurl.com/ycyvzajm. Accessed on 30 April 2023.

food that caters to the carnivores and gluten-free dieters with equal aplomb.

- **Watson's:** This pub is another favourite although nobody is able to articulate why. I suspect that Watson's, like Koshy's, is a beloved Bangalore habit, a memory, a place that you have gone to forever.
- **21st Amendment Gastrobar:** This does all things that Urban Solace used to do but with a lot more space. Different nights, different things—ranging from karaoke, stand-up, disc jockeying, dancing and, of course, Bollywood nights on Saturdays. Forget the food or drinks. Go here to dance.
- **Geist Brewing Co.:** Geist has two outlets, one in Old Madras Road (OMR) and another in Bharatiya Mall. The one at OMR is more atmospheric, while the one at Bharatiya Mall is a lot more spacious.
- **Adda 1522:** Any place that has Paul Fernandes's illustrations on the walls and red oxide floors is someone who knows old Bangalore. This one does pretty cocktails and comfort food.
- **Daysie:** With a bright pink awning and well-priced cocktails, this resto bar just off M.G. Road is patronized by large groups.
- **7Rivers Brewing Company:** Located inside Taj M.G. Road, this is one of the few breweries in star hotels that takes its beer seriously.
- **New BEL Road SOCIAL:** Church Street SOCIAL is still going strong but Riyaz Amlani, the man behind it, has opened a sprawling outlet on New BEL road. Its location makes it a hit and the tested-and-tried formula doesn't fail in the food and drink department.
- **Mirage:** This self-described 'opulent' bar is worth visiting for people-watching, if nothing else. College students go here when they want to dress up a bit, drink and dance.
- **URU Brewpark in J.P. Nagar:** This place has a great selection of Indian gins and a number of well-crafted cocktails in its 17-page-long bar menu.

So, how does this pensioner's paradise-turned-pub city compare with India's other cities? I asked Vikram Achanta, who co-founded '30 Best Bars India'. He said, 'Delhi has more, shall I say pure bars, like PCO, Sidecar, Hoot's and Lair. Mumbai has an outstanding selection of restaurants with great cocktail programs, like Ekaa, Masque, Bastian and Americano. For Bangalore, one definitely hopes for the growth of cocktail culture outside of five-star environs like Copitas and singular outposts like Raahi. The recent opening of Roxie, Boteco and Record Room are good portents for the future.'

Where to Drink Wine in Bangalore

Abhay Kewadkar was the first 'wine person' I met in Bangalore. I still remember the event, even though it occurred over a decade ago. It was organized by the BWC, which currently has about 110 members. The event was held at Taj West End. Kewadkar had set out a series of vials which held various aromatic compounds. We had to smell the compounds and call out what we smelled. I liked Kewadkar instantly because he didn't posture. He spoke in his earthy Maharashtrian accent, interspersed with a French one, when he talked about wine.

I am a member of two wine clubs here in Bangalore—BWC and TWC. The difference between them can be counted in the air-time that wine gets. TWC is a small group. Typically, about 12–15 people meet at different restaurants every month. We spend about three hours talking only about wine. Non-drinking spouses do not accompany us because, as one spouse said, 'How can you people babble non-stop about wine like this?' We take wine seriously, is the somewhat smart-alecky answer. It doesn't make us popular at home.

BWC events are held at glitzy five-star hotels. The wine is decent in terms of value-for-money. There is a lot more socializing which makes it easier on non-drinking spouses. BWC is run by a rotating committee and the quality of events depends on the committee. They do some interesting things—as they have a large membership, they can partner with folks who want to access their membership. Visiting wine brands typically want to do something with BWC. Penfolds showcased their wines at The Ritz-Carlton at a BWC event and Chilean wine brands offered tastings at BWC events before launching their wines in the market. Things like that.

I remember an event that BWC did with Riedel, the wine glass brand, for instance. There was a lovely five-course degustation dinner, followed by a presentation by a visiting European salesman from Riedel. He talked about how the shape of the glass makes a difference to the taste of the wine. I went in rolling my eyebrows, convinced that it was all sales hogwash. To my shock, the same wine smelled different when poured into different glasses— Burgundy glass versus Bordeaux—all Riedel, of course. Naturally, I bought a case after the presentation. Now, they are all broken. If I could, I would buy Zalto wine glasses for everything that I drink but they are too expensive. Farmlore has some very nice wine glasses from Nude. I believe they are the stem-zero ones. I use Lucaris, a Thai brand, at home.

The biggest problem for Indian wine-drinkers is the punishing import duty, which makes accessing good wine difficult. We have a lot of importers who supply to Bangalore, ranging from Wine Park, Sonarys, Aspri, Tetrad and Brindco. I buy from all of them. We all know that we are paying more than double the price for the wine but there doesn't seem to be a way around this issue. Founded by a young couple, the third wine club, Bangalore Wine Trails, offers great value for money at their events held at different restaurants.

The Karnataka Wine Board lists 16 wineries on its website. Grover's website is rather clunky but their reserve wines are good. Their latest range, Signet, has five wines that have been aged in all kinds of new-fangled yet ancient ways—foudre, amphora and concrete. I haven't tried them yet. Kadu is Sula's premium wine made in Karnataka. 'Kadu', which means 'forest' in Kannada, promises to donate a portion of each bottle sold to tiger conservation, so wildlife lovers should buy Kadu Chenin Blanc and Cabernet Shiraz. Big Banyan has tastings for around ₹850 in their winery just outside the city. While you are there, buy their excellent Viognier and Sauvignon Blanc, which are hard to find in retail. SDU Winery's Reserva is what Devesh Agarwal, current BWC President and TWC founder, recommends as a great home-drinking wine. KRSMA Estates always tries to raise the bar with their hard-to-get Shiraz and Sangiovese wines.

If you are new to Bangalore and have some interest in wine, it is a good idea to join these wine groups because they introduce you to an ecosystem. The Trippy Goat restaurant on Cunningham Road is a good place to start because Vishal Nagpal, who runs the place, knows the wine ecosystem from multiple points of view. Abhay Kewadkar, who now runs Tetrad Global Beverages, with Rishad Minochar, has an office in the same complex and often drops by. The French Consulate is down the road, and I have seen the Consul General of France there for lunch.

In terms of wine-friendly fine-dining restaurants, I am afraid I cannot think of too many. The problem is that the markup at five-star hotels for wines is just too high, with a bottle starting at ₹6000 at The Oberoi, The Leela and The Taj hotels. Smaller independent restaurants offer better deals.

Whiskey is the beverage which has Bangalore in thrall. There are many whiskey clubs here, with Amrut and Paul John whiskies being the Indian contenders. Amrut's Greedy Angels was selling globally for $1912 a bottle (when I checked online on *Wine-Searcher*), if you can get it. The erstwhile Israeli Consul General to Bangalore told me that he would have paid double that after tasting it in the Amrut factory. For a Bangalore-brand that is run by the third generation, that's a great thing.

Gin is the drink of the moment. Sipsmith Gin has launched in India but most Indian brands like Greater Than and Stranger & Sons are based in Goa.

So, grab some sourdough bread from Honore Bakery, Sour House or Lavonne. Then, open a bottle and pour yourself a glass. Watch the sunset, eat and drink. That's Bangalore for you!

What is Bangalore's Beer Culture?

It is Saturday night and the Biere Club in Bangalore's Lavelle Road is humming. Young IT professionals down pints of handcrafted ale, lager, wheat and stout beers, all made in-house. 'Bangaloreans enjoy their beer and we thought that it was about time that beer got its due in this city,' says the young and chic Meenakshi Raju, who along with her brother opened the Biere Club. The Rajus belong to a family that is in the hospitality business. 'My father and uncles all own hotels and resorts, so my brother and I wanted to do something different,' she says. It was only after visiting Singapore's Brewerkz that they homed in on a craft brewery. It seemed only fitting for Bangalore—a city that has long been known as the Pub City of India.

Bangalore's salubrious climate, cosmopolitan citizens, colonial buildings and the army cantonments—everything gave this city a faintly British touch, and with it, a strong presence of watering holes. Nostalgic Bangaloreans talk about downing pints of beer at the Windsor Pub, Guzzlers, Scottish Pub and Underground as a rite of passage. Not surprisingly, India's most famous beer brand, Kingfisher, is headquartered in Bangalore. Kingfisher organizes 'The Great Indian Oktoberfest' over three days to promote its range of beers, each appealing to a different price point. 'Beer drinking is so deeply entrenched into the fabric of Bangalore, that I see no way that it could ever be dethroned,' says chef Manu Chandra. 'The good news is that beer is no longer in the male domain, which it was often perceived as. That simply doubles the demographic. It will forever remain a student and youth favourite—that's a substantial number too.'

The IT industry and the disposable income it bestowed on young professionals only increase the demand for beer. Many of them went abroad as engineers, learned to enjoy beer and then returned home to figure out how to duplicate the same thing in India. Narayan Manepally, a beer buff, went abroad and returned to Bangalore. Manepally worked at Intel in Portland, Oregon for many years and brewed beer in his garage. When he returned to take over his family's air-filter business in India, he longed to taste the microbrewed ales that he had enjoyed in the American West Coast. So he co-founded Geist, which they call India's first handcrafted beer. 'The city of Bangalore is like the state of California, which typically sets the trends for the rest of the United States to follow,' he says. 'What we need in Bangalore is a progressive legislation like California that will allow Bangalore to shine to its full potential—opening up markets and levelling the playing field that promotes consumption of lower alcohol drinks like wine and beer.'

Currently, beer in Bangalore, much like other alcoholic beverages, is under the control of the government with crippling regulations over production, distribution and pricing. Beer aficionados have tried importing Trappist and Belgian beer, but even this requires persistence. Despite all the hurdles that the Indian government imposes, beer prevails. 'As a food and beverage professional for over a decade, I was astonished to learn that almost 20 per cent of beverage sales are derived from beer,' says a sommelier at Taj West End. The West End stocks over 450 labels of beer, including Geist's Whistling Wheat and Blonde beers.

Beer's hold over Bangalore might be toppled however, thanks to the popularity of another drink—wine. Says hospitality professional and avid foodie, Aslam Gafoor, 'Today, another drinking culture which is rapidly taking over Bangalore—and the rest of India—is wine. There is a growing tribe of people who are la-di-dahing with a glass of red, rather than being seen dead with a pint. So, in that sense, I am assuming that there is a shift taking place in drinking habits.'

Lending credence to this argument is the presence of many wine clubs including the Bangalore Wine Club, the Wine Society of India, the Bangalore Black Tie and *Food Lovers* magazine's wine dinners, all of which don't serve beer. That said, India has seen a 100 per cent increase in beer consumption, mostly driven by North Indians. Bangalore's beer mavens are more avant-garde and willing to experiment with new microbrewed ales and lagers. 'Personally, I have seen more beer being consumed here than in other cities I have worked in—Hyderabad, Delhi and Kolkata,' says the general manager of ITC Gardenia. 'Bangaloreans love draught beer more than people in other cities and also are willing to try new beers like Trappist Beers and other handcrafted, international beers. Bangalore is also among the first few cities in the country to get a microbrewery.'

Some state governments are making the right noises about lowering taxes and loosening regulations. But still, India has a long way to go. Vendors like Sandeep Bhatnagar, whose company, Ambicon Consultants, markets microbrewery equipment to brewers (Bangalore's Biere Club is a client) have been coaxing the government to align its policies to the present. Bhatnagar lived next to a microbrewery in the UK and now travels all over India in search of good beer.

International brands such as Carlsberg, Tuborg, Budweiser and Fosters are also in the game to sell beer to the vast Indian market. As beer maven, Sanjay Roy says, 'Beer lovers the world over would see themselves as part of a large, worldly, fun-loving tribe. Brand preferences may vary but their love for beer would be a unifying factor.'

His words ring true at the Biere Club pretty much every night where a devoted crew of drinkers down beer, so much so that the place occasionally runs out of a customer's favourite beer.

Bangalore versus
Other Drinking Cultures

I started drinking wine later than most people and, perhaps, as a result, I can afford good wine. I also try to separate the pretentiousness that surrounds this fabled liquid—drunk by the Chinese, first produced in Armenia or Georgia and popularized by the Romans.

I could make a case, and you could argue with me, that the liveliest wine scene in India is in Bangalore. Sure, Delhi has the big spenders.

Mumbai has its clubs and importers too, such as Sanjay Menon of Sansula, who was part of *Decanter* magazine's power list in 2009, and Vishal Kadakia whose firm, Wine Park, sells a number of delicious wines, including a haunting 2014 Honig Cabernet Sauvignon.

Chennai, the gossip goes, has private collectors from the TVS family who have great Burgundy wines. Sadly, I don't know much about Kolkata wine drinkers or collectors but I am very happy to make your acquaintance over a bottle of Château Léoville-Poyferré or any of those natural wines that seem to be the wine-trend of the day.

In Bangalore, there are many clubs that drink wine and whiskey. Two deserve mention—the BWC for its size and longevity and TWC because it is, quite simply, the best wine club in this country.

For non-drinkers such as my husband, wine talk can get tedious. As a result, people who love and want to learn about wine (such as me) are forced to dial back their passion in most social gatherings because after all, where will you find people with whom you can blather on about wine varietals for hours? I discovered that I could do this at TWC. The club meets once a month over dinner. Each member is supposed to bring a bottle and talk about the wine. Others interject with nuggets of information. By the end of the evening, you learn a lot; and if you aren't too drunk, you actually remember it.

My favourite part of the TWC are the themed dinners. Last year, we did a 'first growths' dinner where we tasted the five premier cru wines in succession—Chateau Latour, Lafite, Mouton Rothschild, Margaux and Haut-Brion. We ended the dinner with a divine Yquem, which while not a first growth, is arguably better. We put pen to paper, tasting and describing which wines we liked and why. Was the Margaux better than the Lafite? Why? These were the questions that we had to discuss.

Bangaloreans drink a lot of wine, as members of the BWC can attest. Last year, we had a Russian gentleman from Riedel show us how the same wine tasted different in differently shaped glasses. We swirled and sipped and went from being skeptics to believers.

To paraphrase the great food writer, A.J. Leibling, in order to be a good food writer, you need to have a good appetite. Similarly, in order to be a knowledgeable wine drinker, you need to drink a lot of wine.

If You Want to Drink
Burgundy in Bangalore

Question: How do you organize a Burgundy wine lunch as a collective?
Answer: Very carefully.

Unless you are a collector or a distributor, organizing a wine tasting of great Burgundy is a difficult and expensive proposition. But TWC of Bangalore decided to do just that some time ago. We ended up with quite a line up.

So how can you replicate this? The first is to come up with a theme that works for the wine group. The theme, in turn, is dictated by the wines that are accessible to members of the group. In our case, one member, Ananth Narayanan, had a lot of Burgundy wines. We chose five wines from his cellar and another from the cellar of Devesh Agarwal, co-founder of TWC. The three of us organized the tasting. It took a lot of brainstorming about the line up of the wines and the food-pairing. As always, the trick was to choose the right line up and combination of food and drinks. We initially played around with the idea of tasting the reds first before palate fatigue set in, but we ended up sticking to the classical red-after-white route. We decided to do away with a dessert wine—none of us had a Cremant and we didn't want to compromise on region. We did compromise by beginning the lunch with a 2008 Dom Perignon, even though it is hardly from Bourgogne. We argued a lot about the wines we tasted, but then, isn't that what makes this region special? We ended up with wines that were different varietals and years which lent them to two different types of horizontal tastings.

The first course was a side-by-side blind tasting that we called the 'Clash of the 2009s.' A Louis Latour Corton-Charlemagne Grand Cru versus a Henri Boillet Clos de la Mouchere Monopole Puligny Montrachet. Both were stunning wines with a luscious mouthfeel. Both were savoury with hints of salt and pepper. The Corton had aromas of pear, muskmelons and paired well with brie. The Montrachet smelled of green mustard and a hint of yeast buttermilk. As Sharmila Senthilraja, a member of the TWC said, 'The Corton is like an opera singer, while the Boillet is like a flamenco dancer.'

For the second course, we had a pecorino creme brulee paired with a 2012 William Fevre Bougros Cote Bougros Chablis Grand Cru. Since we had only one such wine, we did a small pour. To me, this Chablis was unlike the other austere ones I have tasted. It was fruity, smelling of violets and grass, quite unlike the minerality that one expects in a Chablis.

For the third and main course, we had a side-by-side blind tasting of three reds—Pinot Noirs—all from the Chambolle-Musigny area. They were a 2003 Frederic Magnien Les Baudes Premier Cru, a 2012 Domaine Georges and Christophe Roumier and a 2011 Domaine Patrice Rion Les Charmes. Since we tasted them blind, it was a fun exercise to figure out which one we liked and whether price was linked to taste. Of the three, the Roumier was most expensive at $393, while the other two were $112 and $100 respectively on *Wine-Searcher*, when I checked. Was the price worth it? Well, that was up to us to decide.

Even though it occupies a tiny part of France, Burgundy or Bourgogne occupies an outsize place in the wine world's imagination. Part of it is because of sheer supply and demand. This region cannot supply enough wine to keep up with the insatiable demand of wine collectors everywhere and, most recently, from China. Part of it has history that is linked to that elusive term, terroir. As Christophe Roumier, who looks after several grand cru labels in Burgundy says in a publicly available YouTube video, terroir happens because a single varietal, the pinot noir is planted in a variety of terrains—the hillsides and lower down—and over several decades. By conducting this controlled experiment, this region has been able to make its vines and wines sing.

How did our wines fare? Well, we all agreed on the wines and gave it points. After the big reveal of which glass carried which wine, this is what we found out:

The Roumier began smelling a little damp. We wondered if it needed more decanting than the three hours that we accorded it. Gradually, it opened up to become the haunting, restrained pinot noir that is eulogized in the movie, *Sideways*. It took a whole hour of swirling in the glass for the wine to truly reveal itself but finally it did; and those of us who waited for it were glad. The Patrice Rion had aromas of fennel, coffee, sour cherry, and, for me, most interesting of all, smoke and cigars. The Magnien was well-structured and epitomized the scents and flavours of what the world imagines a Burgundy wine to possess—cherry, oak, restraint, structure, a good balance of acid and tannins and a long finish.

The TWC has certain rules that make sense. The first rule is that we all share the cost of the wines. We use the website *Wine-Searcher* and get the average price. This is because we don't know how each person has acquired the wine. Some members buy their wines en primeur and get it at a good rate. If the price goes up, they are happy because they get to share their rare and lovely wines with a group of wine-crazy friends and get some of their investment back in return. Some buy it at auction where they don't have control over the price. So, using *Wine-Searcher* is a good way to regulate the prices. After that, Devesh Agarwal, the founder, creates a spreadsheet calculating who has to pay how much based on an equal cost-sharing.

If you have good wines (or good anything for that matter, ranging from clothes to jewellery) cost-sharing based on a democratic and objective measure is a good way to share and improve your pleasure. Wines are meant for sharing, and we found that putting a number on the cost of each bottle helped each member to open up their wine cellars and share their rare wines. Cheers to that.

ARTS AND CULTURE

Where are the Textile Treasures of Bangalore?

The much-loved Vastrabharana comes usually in early October at Chitrakala Parishad. This is the time when saree-lovers of the city will throng to the exhibition to buy their sarees for the year.

I am a Trishanku, by which I mean that I stand between Chennai and Bangalore with respect to my allegiances. But there is one area where Chennai stands head and shoulders above us, and I use this metaphor with reason. That is textiles.

Recently, I learned that the original Vishvakarma exhibition that was held in New Delhi in 1983 had a full 50 per cent of textiles from Tamil Nadu. The remaining states were lumped to the other 50 per cent. Called Pudu Pavu, these Tamil textiles included the amazing Kodali Karuppur, Sikalnayakanpet, Dharmapuri, Thirubuvanam and other weaves. Listen to Sreemathy Mohan and Anita Ratnam talk about the lesser-known weaves of Tamil Nadu on Ratnam's Instagram channel to know more about these weaves.

In contrast, Karnataka's silk weave, the Molakalmuru, is not even worn by Kannada brides, who prefer Kanchipuram to Molakalmuru. Sure, we have our Dharwad drapes and our khadi-weaving clusters, championed by Prasanna and others, but Bangalore lacks a community of crazy-textile-ladies.

In Chennai, gallerist Sharan Apparao holds The Yarn Club lectures. Here, we have the Registry of Sarees but not (yet) a community around it. We have our annual pilgrimage to

Vastrabharana, but, beyond that, the Crafts Council of Karnataka is not a strong presence in the Bangalore 'scene'. Is it because doyennes like Vimala Rangachar, Bharati Govindaraj, Chandra Jain, Geetha Rao, Mangala Narasimhan, Uma Rao and others like them are not 'organizers' who are active on social media? These are quiet, elegant women with a ton of expertise. But in the traditional Indian fashion of *guru-shishya parampara* (teacher-disciple tradition), you have to interact with them one-on-one in order to gain entry into their world of textiles. Today, many of us, including me, get our highs from watching women in beautiful drapes post photos on Instagram. There are folks like Kaveri Ponnappa and Anju Maudgal Kadam who write about sarees. The 100-saree-pact originated in Bangalore. But, beyond that, textile talk is an event, not a feature in Bangalore. There is no community of (younger) women who gather to share expertise, listen to speakers, sell sarees and patronize the weaves.

How do we change this? One way would be for many of the city's saree lovers to join institutions like the Crafts Council of Karnataka, which hosts Vastrabharana. The other is for hoary saree brands in the city to create communities around these weaves. Beloved Bangalore-brands including the House of Angadi and Vimor are making attempts in this direction. Vimor has created a foundation and a museum of living textiles. The House of Angadi has created events that foster a community by inviting speakers to its store. Both these efforts need to go further. I would happily pay to attend textile lectures (that end with some simple oota) that are run like a club. It could happen with a brand or a store like Nalli's which is in Central Bangalore. Newer entrants like Taneira have the clout of the Tata name behind them and a lovely space in Indiranagar. But none of the big saree brands in Bangalore (including the old ones on M.G. Road) do anything consistently. Six events a year at minimum is required to build community. It doesn't have to have celebrity names associated with it. There is a wealth of knowledge within the city. And the point should not be sales—even though that may well happen.

It should be to foster and expand a community of women and men—all of whom are crazy about our woven heritage.

There is some hope. Recently, I attended a talk at the National Institute of Fashion Technology (NIFT). It was put together by sisters Mala and Sonia Dhawan, who tirelessly work in the crafts sector under their banner A Hundred Hands. The panelists included Bangaloreans and textile enthusiasts like Pavitra Muddayya and Prasad Bidapa (who captured Martand Singh in a video interview). Their enthusiasm and knowledge were inspiring. The Director of NIFT Bangalore, Susan Thomas, is dynamic and full of ideas. She and the NIFT team put together a fantastic exhibit titled 'Vignette: Visvakarma Textiles: Art & Artistry,' at the NGMA. When I visited the exhibition, it was heartening to see groups of students walking through and poring over the pieces on the walls. Who knows? Perhaps, it was the beginning of a lifelong love story between a young Bangalorean designer and the handmade textiles that mark this land.

The Spectacular Arts of Karnataka

On 9 December 2022, the Museum of Art and Photography, or MAP, had a soft opening for its patrons and friends, as it geared up for a public opening in early 2023. Like many museums, MAP too began as the obsession of a single man—its founder, art collector Abhishek Poddar. But not all art collectors open museums. For that, you need a specific set of qualities that include passion, relentless drive, subjugation of the ego, a thick skin and a trained eye that sees connections, both artistic and otherwise, across realms. Poddar has this. He knows and loves art, but then many people do. Poddar, by dint of will, put together a collection whose contours became obvious once the museum was fully open. What is obvious is that this is a man who does not give up easily. Bangalore did not make it easy for him. And yet, here we are, a few years later, with the MAP up and running, which in my mind, deserves to be celebrated.

The interesting thing for Bangaloreans is to see what kind of museum MAP will turn out to be over the coming years. How will it evolve?

Every public arts institution in India these days says that it wants to be inclusive but most of them never achieve this goal. A lot of them end up as containers of beautiful objects—a space where an elite few stand silently in contemplation of works of art. Is this where MAP will end up? Or does it want to revert back to the original Latin definition of the word 'museum' which comes from the nine muses of inspiration?

Early museums were places where people gathered to debate and exchange ideas. The famed Mouseion of Alexandria, for example, was a library. Museums, as they stand now, only began in seventeenth- and eighteenth-century Europe. They are Western constructs, which is perhaps why Indians to this day are uneasy about entering museums. A part of the reason behind this reluctance is because we are a privileged civilization where ancient and amazingly beautiful art objects remain a part of our functional everyday lives. In India, we can still enter second-century temples and worship ancient sculptures of gods and goddesses. We can still touch centuries-old murals and walk on stone steps that were built by Chola kings. We don't generally wall off art behind glass and post docents to explain what they mean.

This makes it difficult for museums in general and private museums in particular. Whether it is MAP or KNMA (Kiran Nadar Museum of Art) or even the older Salar Jung Museum, bringing footfalls into the space is a particular problem in India, compared to say, museums in London, which operate within a society that is used to specialized separate spaces quite different from the permeable boundaries that define India. In India, our museums go back millennia, in the form of stupas and temples that plundering kings built to win back public favour. Today, crowds of people happily traipse through Pattadakkal and Badami, quite unaware that the treasures they are touching would be spirited away by modern curators, if they had the chance to do that.

Modern arts institutions, whether they were founded by robber-barons of America or today's rich folks, are acts of passion and redemption; they are a way of equalizing the inequalities that life has so richly bestowed on you, a way to set things right and perhaps, most importantly, leave a legacy. What, then, is the function of a museum in today's India? What is its role and what should be its goal? *Kantara,* the super-hit and must-watch Kannada movie, may offer an answer.

Kantara provided footfalls into movie theatres. Of that, there is no doubt. It did so by being true to its vision, even if that vision was viewed as anti-women, angry-young-man-gone-mad or totally self-obsessed. By showcasing the history and ethos of coastal Karnataka's bhoota kola (a spirit worshipping ritual), *Kantara* brought an esoteric and regional art form into the mainstream. Why he had to portray women in a negative light to achieve this is a question that only *Kantara*'s director, Rishab Shetty, can answer.

So, what will provide footfalls to a museum? I went and looked up the blockbuster exhibits of the Metropolitan and the British museums and they ranged from King Tut to Alexander McQueen.

These may not be relevant to India. What seems to work is a combination of vision plus empathy. You need to have empathy for the people who are entering the premises. What will speak to their soul and spirit? What will nourish their sense of identity and their ideas of beauty? These questions can provide a way forward with respect to the types of exhibits that a museum mounts. If instead, the museum becomes an echo chamber catering to a narrow moneyed group of collectors (as so many have become), it may retain its donors or headlines but it will sag without the essential wild and fierce spirit that flamenco dancers called *duende*.

As a Bangalorean and someone who loves the arts of India, I hope that this city imparts its genteel and welcoming spirit to the arts institutions that call it home.

How Technology Transforms Performing Arts

Here's something. Do you think listening to a concert on Zoom is equivalent to a live performance? Do you think watching a dancer on YouTube will give you the full dimensions of this art? Do you think seeing a painting on a website or app can equate to viewing it face-to-face? The answer to these questions for most of us will be a resounding 'no'. And yet, in this tragedy that Covid is, technology has been our path to cultural consumption. During the lockdown, our engagement with the arts was mostly, if not exclusively, online.

I have watched art offered by Museum of Art and Photography (MAP) online. I have listened to a virtual piano concert organized by the International Music and Arts Society (IMAS). I have attended countless virtual book releases organized by the Bangalore Literature Festival, and done a 3D walkthrough on the Indian Music Experience (IME) digital platform.

The problem is that engaging with the arts virtually gives a feeling of false security. It gives us the feeling that we have absorbed something, even though what we have experienced is a shadow of reality. Technology makes the arts accessible and pervasive, universal and ubiquitous. What it lacks is the immersive emotional depth that only a live experience can give.

So what do we do? Technology is here to stay, even in the intangible cultural realms that lend themselves to collaboration and participation. Today, even *antakshari*[10] jamming sessions happen virtually, with participants from all over Bangalore.

While technology can enhance many experiences—learning a language, for instance, is just as easily done online—it does the performance arts a disservice. To experience the profound emotional resonance of a dance or theatre performance, you have to be there. Performing arts are not portable like books; they are not two-dimensional like films. No, a dance performance demands physical proximity, as does Yakshagana or a theatre show at Bangalore's beloved Rangashankara.

Covid forced performing artists to adapt. Singer Sanjay Subrahmanyan has created and monetized his YouTube channel. Dancer Rukmini Vijayakumar has adapted her performance to the flatness of screen, performing the type of dramatic choreographed works that enhances her reach. Numerous dancers and dance schools are adapting this invasion of technology into their art forms. They are engaging with their audiences in new and unusual ways. Several arts institutions such as Attakkalari Centre for Movement Arts and Natya Institute of Kathak and Choreography (disclosure: I am on their board) offer diploma classes online. Kathak, Odissi and Bharatanatyam teachers, including stalwarts such as Nirupama and Rajendra use social media—Instagram—to teach students and reach new audiences. Bharatanatyam teacher and dancer Praveen Kumar teaches a course on Shaale—a digital learning platform.

About nine years ago, in 2014, I met a young man called Skanda. I wanted to do a Sanskrit podcast which would 'connect the ideas of ancient India with the modern world'. That was the tag line, anyway. I didn't speak Sanskrit but I had just read an article by Aatish Taseer in *Open* magazine called, 'A Historical Sense: What Sanskrit Has Meant to Me.' The piece talked about how Sanskrit opens up India in a way that is beautiful—like the petals of a lotus. Skanda and I brainstormed and created a series

---

[10]An Indian spoken parlour game played as a word chain game with songs.

of episodes for which I interviewed eminent Sanskrit scholars in Seva Sadana in Malleshwaram.

Simultaneously, Skanda was working on his online platform called Shaale which means 'school' in Kannada. He wanted to get the top teachers in music, dance, poetry, literature and more to teach students online via Shaale. Today, Shaale features masterclasses in Bharatanatyam, Carnatic or Hindustani music, Mridangam, Sanskrit poetry from the inimitable Shatavadhani Dr R. Ganesh and much more.

For those of us who live far away and don't have access to excellent teachers, online classes are a godsend. But for those who have access to live teachers, learning online becomes a poor substitute. Online platforms may offer an initiation but they don't connect us to the bones of the art form.

I have a problem with consuming culture virtually. I especially dislike how technology has converted live performances into flat-screen replicas. All mediums change the form. Technology, for the most part, diminishes the performing arts.

The best way to enjoy the sheer physicality, presence and immediacy of dance is in person. In Bangalore, this is possible in multiple venues: Chowdiah Hall, Gayana Samaja and others. So what are you waiting for?

Raining Books in Bangalore

It is raining books in Bangalore. Well, our rains have increased as well, particularly during the festive season when shoppers wade through puddles and storm drains to buy their mango leaves, fruits and flower garlands at Sampige Road in Malleshwaram.

Bookstores are beloved in Bangalore. Church Street is where some of the good ones are located. My favourite is Blossom Book House, where you can spend an afternoon browsing the shelves. The owner Mayi Gowda knows all the books that he has and can point you to the right shelf if you want books on 'design' or 'tarot cards'.

Book clubs abound as well. One of my favourites is Cubbon Reads and the Cubbon Book Club, but pretty much every neighbourhood or building colony has a book club.

Despite that Bangalore has not become a character in books or movies the way Mumbai has. Lavanya Sankaran's books had glimpses of this city. Acclaimed ecologist Dr Harini Nagendra, whose earlier book *Nature in the City* mixes history with sustainability, has come up with a delightful series called *The Bangalore Detectives Club*, featuring a saree-wearing sleuth. The series, set in 1920s Bangalore, is a must-read for newer Bangaloreans who don't understand the nostalgia that old Bangaloreans feel for this beautiful city.

Prolific author Andaleeb Wajid promotes other Bangalore authors like Anuja Chauhan, Bijal Vachharajani and Aruna Nambiar in her Substack newsletter. Her own books are Bangalore's answer to those Harlequin romances we all read on a rainy afternoon.

Try her latest, *Accidentally Married,* if you are in the mood for romance.

Books can be a universal and a private pleasure. Platforms like the Bangalore Literature Festival, Neev Literature Festival, Atta Galatta and the book clubs that proliferate in this city try to juggle heavyweights like Sudha Murty and Ramachandra Guha with emerging voices such as Sabin Iqbal and Manu Bhattatiri— always a 'fine balance'.

Some platforms like the New India Foundation and the BIC have made Bangalore their home but don't make a conscious effort to root themselves in this soil. Some authors do. Paul Fernandes's work, for instance, gives new Bangaloreans an excellent introduction to what this city has lost and gained. Zac O'Yeah writes about Majestic, which is to Bangalore what Grand Central Station is to New York. But many other authors like Vikram Sampath and Anita Nair are from Bangalore but their books are not about this city. Does that matter?

Can Bangalore as a city inspire tales, stories, books, films and more—in the way that London and New York have done, or Florence did during the Renaissance? Can Bangalore aspire to be a cultural capital with a vivid throbbing heart? What does it take for a city to provide inspiration to authors? What does it take for a city to foster the creative ferment?

Creative output is hard to engineer and even harder to manage. It is an ineffable thing that happens over decades and requires a confluence of factors in order to flower. The Rennaissance, for instance, began in Florence because of patronage from the Medici family, the migration of Greeks with their manuscripts to Italy after Constantinople fell, and most importantly, educators who wanted to teach the citizenry to speak, write and read the humanities.

Bangalore has immigrants in spades but most are economic immigrants who come here to launch start-ups. It has patronage from the city's elite. What it lacks is a citizenry that are interested in debating and discussing the humanities and arts. We lack the classical Bengali 'adda' culture, which is perhaps why Kolkata and

Mumbai are the two Indian cities which are closest to creating a cultural ferment.

That can change for Bangalore. The origin of the word 'rennaissance' was the Italian *rinascita*, which means 'rebirth' or 'revival'. Post-Covid (fingers crossed), several organizations are trying to create addas in Bangalore. Virtual addas don't count in my opinion. You need physical presence, people meeting in person for ideas to have sex and create new forms. Design Friday, a club run by entrepreneur Sujata Keshavan, used to do that.

The other necessary factor for creative ferment is that the clubs or addas cannot be pan-Indian and 'place-less' like Algebra Conversations. They require a membership. The same folks need to show up again and again in one location—like what happens in Koshy's or Blossom bookstore.

There are rumblings that this may happen in Bangalore. There is talk of a discussion club which brings together the same group of people in a closed-door format. Every cultural institution in Bangalore needs to have a version of this, ideally with a mixed bag of people. Rangashankara, MAP, Takshashila, BIC, Indian Music Experience, Gayana Samaja and others can be the vessel in which creativity can boil over.

The question is: is it time for Bangalore's renaissance to begin?

Is There Hope for Bangalore's Heritage Buildings?

Rishad Minocher calls himself a hospitality consultant but he is really an epicurean who enjoys single malts, fine wine, good food and heritage buildings. He happens to live in one—a 175-year-old gem situated in the centre of Bangalore on Cunningham Road. Called Hatworks Boulevard, the one-acre property has now been converted into a series of high-end boutiques and retail outlets. Minocher and his wife, Anna, live in the back with their two daughters. 'My grandfather rented it from the original owner, a British man, and then bought it after the Second World War,' says Minocher. 'After my parents passed, we five siblings were left with a choice. Should we give it to real estate developers who would tear it down or construct a high-rise in its place or figure out another way? We chose the other way.'

Minocher and his wife travelled all over Asia and saw Chinese shop-houses being used as retail outlets in Singapore, Malaysia and Thailand. They decided to do the same with their home with an iron-clad contract to all prospective tenants. No major structural changes were allowed; and several architectural features could not be touched—the heritage flooring, mud brick walls, lime plaster, curlicues above the entrance arch reflecting the family's Parsi heritage and the Burma teak false ceiling—all had to be handled with care by the tenants. Even fixtures like air-conditioning units had to be inserted tastefully and not 'be stuck here and there so that they are an eyesore,' as Minocher says.

Several years into the exercise, Minocher says that the family is happy with their decision. 'We have the home to enjoy and leave for future generations. It is a great way to keep these old structures going. Even financially, the rent we are getting is commensurate with the rentals in the area,' he says.

Heritage preservation in Bangalore has finally come to the fore, thanks to an unusual confluence of visionary architects, civic activists and a young workforce that has become wealthy thanks to the software boom. This resolutely modern city, known more for its call centres and IT companies, has large tracts of army land and several buildings from the Colonial era.

In the '80s, this city expanded and exploded, thanks to a nascent software industry. Homeowners who lived in old bungalows with their characteristic monkey-top windows and slanting tiled roofs were forced to make a choice. As the land they lived on became more and more expensive, many sold it to real estate developers who tore down old bungalows and built high-rise monstrosities in their place. A few homeowners, however, chose to do what architects call 'adaptive reuse', i.e. turning their homes into offices, shops and in one case, the National Gallery of Modern Art or NGMA.

The NGMA building used to be the home of Raja Manickavelu Mudaliar. The Mudaliars are an Indian 'forward-caste' community with extensive land holdings in Bangalore. They came from neighbouring Tamil Nadu during the British time to service the British army cantonments with leather and oil goods—they could touch leather while their Brahmin counterparts wouldn't—and never left. Two of the nicest homes on M.G. Road in Bangalore are still owned by people in the Mudaliar community.

The Velu family remains prominent and one of their homes is now a luxury boutique called Raintree. The patriarch, Raja Manickavelu, lived in a sprawling three-acre mansion on Palace Road. Minocher remembers stories from his mother who used to visit the mansion for dinner parties served in the family's exquisite gold dinner-set. In the sixties, the state government acquired the mansion, and in 2000, decided to house Indian art in its lofty premises. Architectural firms were invited to bid for the complex project involving landscaped gardens, a crumbling colonial mansion and painstaking restoration. The architect who won the project was Naresh Narasimhan.

Naresh shepherded the controversial and complicated project through to completion. Competing architects carped that Naresh had won the commission unfairly; artists complained that they were not consulted in the design of the gallery spaces. Nine years later, in February 2009, the gallery was finally opened to the public.

Since that landmark project, Naresh has developed his nascent passion for restoration and has turned into a spokesperson for the city's architectural heritage. His father, also an architect, was involved in Bangalore's first heritage preservation project. The city wanted to tear down the fire-engine red Attara Kacheri landmark building. 'My Dad and his colleagues did something very smart,' says Naresh. 'They invited the prominent English conservation architect Sir Bernard Feildon (responsible for restoring Britain's cathedrals, the Taj Mahal and the Great Wall of China) to come in and speak to the city officials. Feildon persuaded them to let the building stay, thankfully. It was a great victory for the conservation lobby in those days.' Today, the Attara Kacheri building houses the Karnataka High Court.

But such public heritage buildings are few and far between in Bangalore. They do exist; but far more common are gated estates like Palm Meadows and Epsilon with homes modelled on Californian villas with palm trees and three-car garages. 'Maybe we have too much of history in India and, therefore, very little respect for it,' says Naresh in explanation. 'Historical buildings are seen as old-fashioned and out of date. There is no appreciation of the physicality of buildings; no understanding that unless these buildings are preserved, the history of the city and the continuation of its fabric is lost. India's old buildings are seen as archeology, not history; and there is a difference.'

There has been some cause for hope. Groups like Heritage Beku (We Want Heritage) have been pushing for better conservation and restoration of Bangalore's heritage buildings. Successive state governments talk about establishing a 'heritage cell' within the municipal corporation that would look into three areas—built heritage, natural heritage and cultural heritage. Such a move would be lauded by naturalists and ornithologists like M.B. Krishna.

Bangalore is one of India's few cities that has large lakes such as Ulsoor Lake and Hesarghatta Lake. If implemented, the government's heritage cell will look to preserve not just old buildings but also Bangalore's lakes, traditional and scenic neighbourhoods such as Malleshwaram and Basavanagudi and its parks.

Currently, Lalbagh and Cubbon Park are Bangalore's two large green spaces. Krishna thinks that the way forward is to get multinationals involved in preserving Bangalore's green heritage. 'Companies like IBM, Bausch and Carrefour come into India and try to create the temperate landscapes that they are used to in their home countries within their Indian corporate campuses,' says Krishna. 'Instead, they could use native trees which would not only grow quickly and flourish in Bangalore's climate but also reduce their landscaping costs as well. Carrying the argument further, they could try to incorporate architectural elements like cross ventilation and lattice-work that are more suited to a tropical climate instead of building glass-and-steel towers that use more energy and electricity.'

The good news for Bangalore is that a dedicated band of naturalists, architects and civic planners are making a concerted effort to not only influence the government but also gain public support. 'The real challenge is to educate people that old buildings are not bad buildings and they just need some TLC,' says Naresh. 'We need to come up with a way to make them relevant to modern use.'

If only Bangalore's real estate developers would jump on the heritage bandwagon, but such 'enlightened developers,' as Minocher says, are an 'oxymoron'.

A Flavour of Bangalore's
Distinctive Art World

It was yet another opening at Gallery Sumukha, founded in Bangalore in 1996. About 200 people crowded into the space, discussing the art and sharing opinions. What was distinctive about this group? The absence of anyone from the IT industry for one. 'We have never had anyone from the IT industry visit our gallery or buy our work,' said owner, Premilla Baid. 'We've always wondered why. Do they support other things like theatre or do they simply not connect to the art and culture scene in Bangalore?'

Bangalore's art scene is still nascent compared to Delhi or Mumbai. In the '60s and '70s, influential artists such as K.K. Hebbar moved out of the city to gain fame. In the '80s, artists such as S.G. Vasudev, Balan Nambiar, Yusuk Arakkal and Gurudas Shenoy laid down roots in Bangalore and infused imaginative regionalism into the framework of Indian modernist art. They used spirituality, crafts and folk idioms in their work, showing largely outside Bangalore. Government museums such as the Karnataka Chitrakala Parishath (CKP) and Venkatappa Art Gallery (VAG) were viewed as old-fashioned moribund institutions.

That is slowly changing in Bangalore now. Sure, the city has quirky galleries and museums such as a Brain Museum (displaying brains in various stages of healthy and decay with free guided tours at the National Institute of Mental Health and Neurosciences or NIMHANS); a cartoon gallery near M.G. Road; a philatelic museum of stamps; a military museum which seems obvious given that a whole area was once an army cantonment; the Indian Music Experience, a space dedicated to understanding and appreciating music in innovative ways (a recent exhibit was on bird songs); and most recently, MAP. Says Baid, 'The opening of MAP has created a buzz for Bangalore and hopefully that will carry into the future.'

Gallery Sumukha's roster includes well-established Bangalore-based artists such as Pushpamala, Shantamani, Ravi Kumar Kashi, B.V. Suresh, Cop Shiva (that's his name), and others. There are other galleries including KYNKYNY, Crimson, Gallery G, Time & Space among others. In the last few years, the NGMA has tried to enliven the cultural conversation with lectures, tree walks, poetry readings and curated shows. The best part of the NGMA, however, might well be its beautiful grounds and the heritage mansion that it occupies.

The more exciting stuff is happening on the streets with artist collectives such as Jaaga and 1Shanthiroad, offering residencies for artists from all over the world. The Rangoli Art Centre provides street-level art below the M.G. Road metro line. Since Bangalore has a combination of scientists, tech folks and artists, it results in unusual combinations including dance performances mixing Artificial Intelligence (AI) and climate change, which happened under the banner, BeFantastic.

The word that is most often used to describe the Bangalore art scene is 'non-commercial', given that it is not as market-driven as India's other metros. Relative to Delhi and Mumbai, rents are reasonable. The city does not have too much of a celebrity culture. Discussions in the art world don't centre around 'who came and bought what', as an ex-country head of Sotheby's India said. Bangalore in that sense, evokes an art community that existed in other Indian metros but has since been forgotten or left behind.

'The kinds of work that Bangalore artists make is somehow bolder and reminds me of an earlier time in Bombay—when I came out of art school', said artist Sudharshan Shetty whose family is from the area and visits Bangalore frequently. 'To do what you like because there is no market pressure is a gift.'

It is a gift that is hard-won given the paucity of patronage. An exception is 1Shanthiroad Studio/Gallery. Founded by Suresh Jayaram, it is a nurturing yet cutting-edge space in the city. On a typical day, artists wander in and out of the house located under a large leafy tree. Unusual exhibits about queer perspectives, trees, bondage and gender are showcased. I attended a talk some years ago where writer Achal Prabhala showed a series of horror and porn movies from Pakistan. The packed audience included saree-clad grandmothers mingling with hipsters in low-waisted jeans smoking cigarettes. 'Bangalore doesn't have enough of anyone in any field for specialized cliques to form,' Prabhala said. 'So the poets, artists and writers are forced to socialize with each other.'

Although Bangalore has an art market, the stakes are not high and prices are relatively low. This allows for fellowship and camaraderie between artists, said Malavika P.C., who along with Sandeep T.K., coordinates the programming at 1Shanthiroad. She further adds, 'Bangalore is the hub of art in South India. It is not a clique; it is very open. People share their art practices and are happy to answer questions. There are so many collectives that make sculpture, prints, installations and photographs. In fact, the whole city practises art and you cannot say that about too many metropolitan cities.'

Bangalore's Identity Crisis with Respect to the Arts

Musicians, like all artistes, are a breed apart. They enjoy external perks—standing ovations, packed concert schedules, income, and yes, alas in the younger breed, product endorsements. Still, it is possible, especially among the older generation, to find musicians who practise their art just for the sheer pleasure of it—for that particular bliss attained from singing a morning raga at dawn in solitude.

We Indians have always revered our musicians. When my guru sings a note, he sings it with such wholeness of intent that every note becomes imbued with perfection. It is like blowing a bubble and watching it suspended mid-air. For a moment, you forget yourself and the world; you are transported to another realm.

For many Indians of today, reality is measured in numbers—third-quarter profits, advertising revenues and bottom line. Musicians, on the other hand, live in a world that is entirely intangible and immeasurable. How does one put a value to the beauty of the Raga Kapi sung by someone who knows it intimately? How does one put a price on an hour spent with such a person? Musicians, artists and poets allow us a glimpse into this parallel but completely blissful universe where the measure of a human is not in numbers, but in the perfection of a musical phrase, gesture of a paint-stroke, cadence of a verse or shape of a raga. Being in their company is a gift; it's like a boost of pure oxygen.

The state of Karnataka, where I live, is the womb of Carnatic music. The music scene here isn't as vibrant as neighbouring

Chennai, particularly in December. But here too, there are sublime concerts, offered for free throughout the year. Come March and the Ramaseva Mandali concert series begins. This concert series has been conducted by the same family for 70 years. The father started the tradition and now his four sons and their families have taken over. The four sons, daughters-in-law and grandchildren all live together in a large rambling house in old Bangalore. All of them hold day jobs and run businesses. But in March, they put it all aside for the concert series, which is held in a big tent in Chamrajpet, an old Bangalore neighbourhood.

I love attending these concerts for many reasons. The music can be soul-elevating or merely competent. As a feminist, I like to watch women compete on an equal playing field. Carnatic music offers a level playing field for musicians of all genders. Some of the most popular artistes are women—crowd pullers such as Aruna Sairam, Bombay Jaishree, Ranjani Gayathri, Sowmya, Sudha Raghunathan and Nithyashree. In the hierarchy of Carnatic concerts, they command equal stature and fees as the men. This is nice to see. Also nice to watch is the play of tradition against pioneering change—Sukanya Ramgopal, for instance, is one of the few women playing the *ghatam*—a clay pot that is harder to play than its cousin, the tabla. Earlier, women did not play percussion instruments on stage. Now, there are several women who do so. This, to me, is the new India—change pitted against tradition.

The Ramaseva Mandali concerts are sponsored by banks and consumer-goods companies—State Bank of Saurashtra, State Bank of Mysore and Karnataka Soaps, to name a few. No multinational or IT company in sight, yet the concert series is thriving. At the end of one concert, the sponsor—who happened to be the marketing manager of Mysore Sandalwood Soap—went on stage to honour the artistes. He put a garland of roses around their necks. Then he did something that shocked me, fresh as I was from egalitarian America—he touched their feet. A distinguished gentleman, probably twice as old and earning four times as much as the young musicians on stage; yet he paid his respects to their art by touching their feet. This, to me, is Indian culture.

Every April, the Odakathur Mutt in the Ulsoor neighbourhood I live in holds their music concert series. This year too, the best talents from largely the southern states will grace the stage. I, along with hundreds of people, will sit on the floor and listen to transporting music—music that will offer a glimpse of the cosmos.

LIFE AND LIVING

How to Get Things Done in Bangalore

When you move to a new city, the most common dilemma is how to get things done. You need to change your driver's license, buy and register a home and a car. The list goes on. How easy or difficult is it to do this in Bangalore? And do you need to grease the wheels?

The answer to both is yes, but not in the way that you might imagine. When my husband went to register his company, for example, the killer app that he discovered for all negotiations was numerology. He didn't want to pay a bribe. When the government official senses such reluctance, he or she has only one choice—to make life difficult by prolonging the time or posing obstacles. To both, a good answer is numerology.

When the officer behind the desk said that the name of the company had to be changed because it didn't conform to the rules (a blatant lie), my husband's response was, 'Sir, but my astrologer said that this is numerologically correct.' To his shock, the officer accepted the explanation.

Similarly, a female officer said that she couldn't sign the files because she needed more documents. 'Return next week,' she ordered. His reply? 'Madam, today is a *shubha muhurtha* (auspicious day). I will ask my colleague to bring the documents now itself and will wait however long for you to sign.' Again, she was stymied and had no response. After a few hours of making him wait, she did sign the papers.

The next question is about bribing officials for approvals.

In this, there is a fork. Some people are philosophically against bribes, and, perhaps, we all should be. Some are pragmatic and believe that this is the only way to get things done in India. How about a compromise? How about a gift package containing an educational book, chocolates and a metre of fabric? A friend does this. The rationale is that this is a donation towards a good cause. The educational book will educate a child—specifically, the RTO (Regional Tranport Office) officer's child. The chocolates? Well, they can be shared by all the peons in the office. As for the fabric? That is a multi-purpose solution to many problems. It could, for example, be used to cover the dusty files in the RTO office. In that sense, my friend's gift is a service to the country. It conforms to American President John F. Kennedy's famous question, 'Ask not what your country can do for you; ask what you can do for your country.' Is it a bribe? Yes and no. Does it get your license re-registered to Karnataka? Yes.

Once you settle down, you need a steady supply of things which are easy to find today because social media knows more about your likes and dislikes than your own mother. Its algorithms curate a list of delectable objects and things you can buy, ranging from clothes, makeup and footwear to organic strawberries, composting pots and vegan handbags. All you need to do is click on what you see, order and buy it.

But there is one area where social media will not help at all and that is tailoring. If you, like me, believe that the pleasure of living in India is access to bespoke tailoring, you need to find a tailor fast and one who will work with you. Find one within your area. That is the easiest. But I know women who come all the way to Commercial Street to get their clothes stitched because it contains a concentration of talent and fabric material. You need to know how to work with these busy folks, particularly in the festive season, because ladies, you know that come Diwali, Christmas or Ramadan, the most important man in your life is not the spouse who stuns you with flowers or the secret lover who sizzles in bed or the son who cajoles you with puppy-eyes or the boss who is your card to that promotion. It is the tailor who will stitch a 'katori-cut' blouse that will make you look like Tabu. So, how does one find the right tailor?

First of all, the question is wrong. You don't need 'a' right tailor. You need 'ten' right tailors because the sad truth is that they will all fail you at some point and you will need an out. The trick with negotiating with tailors is that you need to be able to threaten and follow through. There is no point in saying, 'Give it a week before Ramadan or I will go elsewhere,' if you have no backup. The second thing to realize is that these are temperamental artisans who you should not threaten. Instead, you should cajole them. You should do some drama, tell them stories about how a wedding is happening in the family and you want—no—you *need* to wear the blouse that he has stitched because it is the only thing that works in your life. Shed a few tears and watch the magic happen.

The same thing applies for every repair person who enters your home to fix the toilet, the curtains or loose doors. Sure, you have to negotiate the price and try to get them to deliver within a certain time, but at some point, you have to call the shots. 'This does not work for me. Let me find someone else,' you have to say. And mean it.

That is when things will happen. Indians, you see, are masters of brinksmanship. You see it in our roads where trucks will come straight at you, expecting you to get out of the way. In such situations, you cannot blink and fall for the threat. You too have to go full blast and move straight ahead till either he or you swerve at the last minute and hope that you don't hit the nearby cyclist who is doing his own version of brinksmanship.

Life under Lockdown
in Bangalore

So what's your Covid story? By now, it must have hit home or close to home—people you know, people you admire, people who are family, people who are iconic to Bangalore. Like T.S. Shanbhag, owner of the fabled Premier Book Shop, who died of Covid on 4 May 2021. Or Someshwar Shyam Sunder, a 'forest giant' felled by Covid. Or S.G. Neginhal, a man who knew the trees and forests of Karnataka, also felled by Covid. The list goes on.

For those of us who were lucky enough to sit indoors during the lockdown, life played out on social media. Words were currency and were used to secure oxygen, medicines and hospital beds. WhatsApp forwards no longer had the halo of altruism that they sometimes come with. 'Look at me. Here I am trying to help humanity. Aren't I virtuous?'

No, in those days, messages were raw and vulnerable pleas and entreaties to the world about saving your children, family and friends. The requests themselves were terse and desperate.

'My son needs Remdesevir. We bought one for ₹20,000. We need five more. Anyone willing to sell?'

'Is it true that a South Bangalore politician stormed into a hospital and forcibly took all the oxygen cyclinders there? What is this—minimum governance, maximum government?'

'My SpO2 is just about 84. Should I do pronal breathing? Can someone teach me?'

'Ambulances don't come. Don't rely on them. Use Swiggy and

Dunzo for medicines. They have really come through in a way that this government hasn't.'

'Someone please convince my Mom to get vaccinated. She is doing cow urine, water pulling and steaming.'

At least in India, people who are anti-vaccine are so because they are scared of the side-effects or because they trust alternative remedies. In the US, I know people who are anti-vaccine because they feel that the government is 'chipping' them, i.e. inserting little chips into their body with the vaccine so that they can get all their personal data.

India has a Marxian approach to death. When the World Health Organization (WHO) said that India had the 'capacity' to withstand a pandemic, what they meant is that Indians take death lightly. If 300 people die in a train accident in Switzerland, it is a catastrophe that will be analysed and solved so that it is never repeated. In India, deaths are merely a Stalinesque statistic.

My story begins at midnight with a call from a friend. We had been monitoring her for days after she complained about having fever. She was in her early forties and had not been vaccinated. The fever continued. The pulse oximeter showed that her oxygen levels were dropping. Finally, a few of us rallied around and insisted that she go to the hospital. She had family—a husband and two small children. They were all scared. The husband telephoned every hospital in the vicinity and the city. There were no vacant hospital beds. By then, his wife needed to go into the Intensive Care Unit. Her oxygen levels were not rising. Around five of us—friends and family—worked the phones. We put out messages and got many false trails that lead nowhere. *Use this app to find a bed*, said someone. Not true. *Call this number*. Nobody picked up.

Finally the husband found a small hospital in Jayanagar that was willing to admit his wife—not into the ICU as there was already a patient in their one-bed ICU—but in the general ward. We admitted our friend in the hospital and watched over her for a day. No improvement. She needed to be transferred into the ICU. But, luckily, the patient who was occupying the

ICU was discharged. That single ICU in our city of millions saved her life—not because it was available when she needed it but because her body had the good luck to hold off for a day before degenerating.

From an evolutionary perspective, the people who were perishing were taking the heat of the virus; sacrificing themselves in a way because they were taking the strongest strains of this virus to their graves. Gradually, the virus became weaker, or so evolutionary biologists said.

So what now? We live in the age of the virus. Second and third waves are a textbook case of every pandemic. The Indian government ignored this rudimentary fact. Instead of preparing, it presumptuously and falsely claimed that it had vanquished the virus. Instead of gathering and distributing vaccines centrally, India practised vaccine diplomacy by sending vaccines to neighbouring countries when it hadn't served its own citizens. In early March, the government's own Covid committee warned the government about the second wave. Busy with election rallies in West Bengal, Tamil Nadu and Kerala, the central government passed the buck to the states—leaving each state scrambling for and fighting against each other for vaccine allocations. What should have been a coordinated, consistent and centralized effort became a chaotic carnival instead that made India the laughing stock of the world.

Bangalore suffered, as did most of India. It was left to the citizens to pick up the pieces and do what the government ought to have done—govern.

How to Exit a WhatsApp Group

My friend, Raju, is incensed. He calls me out of the blue and says, 'I am thinking of exiting too.'

I know exactly what he is talking about. Our high school WhatsApp group has become a battlefield. In one day, six people have abruptly exited the group.

Some left after a few principled words (which were immediately construed as sanctimonious holier-than-thou natter by the people at whom the words were aimed). 'Those of you who have been defending this government ought to ask yourself if you will take such a strong position if one of your own died in the hospital without a bed, oxygen or care.'

Others left with a virtual throw of arms in the air. 'Folks, I am tired of this infighting. Will return when things get saner in our group. Thank you all and have a great life.'

Raju's phone call is really a plea. He doesn't want to leave the group but he wants the fighting to stop.

'Can you mute those two jokers?' he asks. 'After all, you are the admin.'

I know the two people he is talking about. They have hijacked the conversation so that everything is about forwarding articles that support their position.

I attempt a mild plea. 'The rest of us can change the discourse. Why can't you change the topic? Talk about Danish Sait or the latest Kannada movie? Why are you keeping quiet and letting them have at it?

'What's the use? The two of them just rant and rant. There is no air-time for anything else.'

The trouble with what seemed like a never-ending, ever-complicated pandemic was that people got testy and wanted to place the blame somewhere.

These days, there is enough blame to go around. We want to blame someone for the vulnerability that we all feel. The illusion of control that we all had about our lives has now been irrevocably shattered. Today, we live and breathe because a tiny virus decides not to invade our body.

Bangalore, like most of the country, was teetering under wave after wave of the mutating virus. Battle lines had been drawn and they were as obvious as the *Lakshmana rekha*[11] that our politicians keep talking about. There were the pro-BJP and the anti-BJP folks.

As is the case with any large WhatsApp group, there were participants who belonged to both camps. And they could not stand each other, even if they once played gully cricket together. The result? A potent brew of sarcasm, vicious name-calling and principled outrage. The stakes, meanwhile, were dug deeper and deeper into the ground. And unlike a battlefield, there were no clear winners. Each side thought that they were right. 'Obviously,' they said, with a roll of the eyes and a sneer.

It didn't used to be this way. Bangalore was a different kind of city. Whatever the reason, I haven't felt the extreme kind of reaction during the 15 years that I have lived in Bangalore, that happens frequently, in say, neighbouring Chennai. Even road rage borders on civil here.

So, what do you do? How do you deal with the cacophony of WhatsApp groups? How do you deal with people who once used to be your friends but have now morphed into folks you can barely stand? How do you keep the vitriol out of the conversation? Do you make a principled and abrupt exit or not? Do you engage or mute the whole conversation?

---

[11]Taken from the Ramayan, in modern parlance, Lakshmana Rekha (Lakshman's Line) refers to a strict convention or rule.

This wasn't the case only in Bangalore though. WhatsApp has always been geography-agnostic. Most of the school and college groups that we are a part of have participants from a number of metros all over India and abroad. On one hand, it is exhilarating to be in this giant adda. On the other, it is exhausting to just keep up with the barrage of messages. One of my friends exited all her WhatsApp groups two months ago. It is something I think about every day.

A way forward was afforded by Deepa Krishnan, who lives in Mumbai. In a long post on—what else—Facebook, she talked about how she used to be one of those abrupt exiters but eventually made her way back into the groups that she exited to figure out how to tolerate the folks whose opinions she was against. 'It's not easy, the process of learning to tolerate someone who is the opposite of you and whose very presence is constantly pushing your buttons,' she said. 'I really struggled a lot. I still struggle but it is getting easier. What made it possible was the realization that the group was a community in which I lived (albeit virtually). Communities are made up of all kinds of people, just like the real world around me. I deal with a lot of diverse people in the real world, without getting into fights. Then, surely, I could do the same in the virtual world?'

To clamp down on voices that present views opposite of your own is a slippery slope. If one of the pillars of democracy is free speech, it also ought to be a part of our lives. After 20 minutes of good-natured ribbing, I eventually talked Raju off the cliff that he had climbed on. We both agreed that there were two ways to deal with WhatsApp triggers—to speak louder and take over the conversation or to stay silent and ignore the fighters.

Sanity has to come back sometime. To the world and to the virtual world.

Infighting in Bangalore Apartment Complexes

The 'tiny' virus taught us many things. The illusion of control that we all thought we had about our lives has now been irrevocably shattered. The virus showed us the extent of our own fallibility; and how the rivers and animals that we once viewed as sacred and since desecrated can mutate and fight back in ways we cannot even imagine.

Social distancing created emotional distances and the mental health issues that emerged out of the pandemic are still hard to know or measure.

For me, one of the biggest lessons that the virus taught was about normalcy. One person's normal is another person's outrage. This gets compounded in a residential community that can only enforce norms, not laws. Requests, not rules.

In 1620, the French polymath Blaise Pascal said, 'People are usually more convinced by reasons they discover themselves than by those found by others.' This applies to norms and rules surrounding this virus as well.

How did your community deal with social distancing? Were all of your friends and neighbours on the same page? It was not so in my community.

Bangalore in May 2021 had the dubious distinction of being the top city in terms of active Covid cases. In mid-May, we had close to six lakh active cases. As the city administration faltered, most apartment communities had to come up with rules of their own. And this is where the variety of responses to rules were on wide display.

Take my own community. With 64 apartments, we are not especially large. During the lockdown imposed by the city government pretty much all through May, the volunteer committee that runs our building complex came up with what they thought of as a fairly sensible rule. They banned domestic workers, drivers and other external service people from entering our community.

This, I must add, was the norm in many large gated communities in Bangalore. What happened afterwards was a display of the Indian mindset.

Indians, as a rule, hate to be told what to do. Although, this isn't a uniquely Indian trait—most people don't like to be dictated to—the difference is that Indians are very creative and imaginative when it comes to breaking rules. Worse, they think that rules apply to everyone else except them.

When domestic workers were banned in our apartment, many of my neighbours who I thought I knew came up with novel ways to circumvent this rule. One spirited the worker into the basement in her car and into her apartment. Another fought with the security guards every morning, heaping abuse on them for preventing the worker from entering. A third announced that she would take responsibility if any person entering her home infected the community.

This was the opposite of an idle threat. This was an idle responsibility. There was no way that this lady would take charge of our building in case her employee infected the rest of us.

In the 1950s, social psychologist Leon Festinger came up with what he called the 'theory of cognitive dissonance.' Humans hate to hold two thoughts that are in conflict with each other. So, the household that cannot do without their workers does not like to hear from their neighbours that they could be carriers of infection. Their response is to double down and insist that they are right and that others are overreacting.

The same applies to parents in a school, workers in a factory and employees in a company. How, then, do we protect a community?

When you have to rely on good faith and social norms to

influence good behaviour, it becomes an exercise in persuasion. In India, social distancing is an alien concept. Our homes have fluid boundaries, with people coming in and going out. During Bangalore's lockdown, there were families in my community who decided to do without any help—no housekeepers or drivers. And there were families who simply couldn't do without them. How to get these two extremes on the same page?

In the birdwatching group that I am part of, there are members who believe that going for nature outings is okay as long as all members wear masks. And there are others who believe that such gatherings are very risky. 'Each to his own' may work under normal circumstances but not when you are steering an unruly ship.

Values are a nebulous thing. What might hold strong and true for you might seem strange and shifty to others. Do you eschew all outside food or do you order in and say that you will support local businesses? Both views have merit in this situation. Do you gather outdoors with a few friends or not? Do you get vaccinated or not?

What seems to work is the well-placed question, the suggestion without aggression. As Abraham Lincoln once said, in order to persuade people, you have to first befriend them. If this approach worked for a man who had to heal and bring an entire country together, why not try it in your community?

Is There Hope for Bangalore's Roads?

If you are asthmatic, don't come to Bangalore. If you have dust allergies, this ain't the place for you. If you have balance issues, be especially careful as you pick your way through the mounds and valleys that have now become common here.

Bangalore's streets are like moon craters. Why bother with Mars rovers, I say, when you can barely walk on Magadi Road?

Every subsequent government digs up the streets, seemingly all at the same time in an effort to 'improve' the city.

For a citizen, this ham-fisted process is the opposite of user-friendly. They seem to be digging up all the roads in sequence, instead of finishing the work section-by-section. As a result, the whole city looks like a MGNREGA[12] exercise gone wrong. Migrant construction workers sit on sidewalks with their cute children who play on the mounds of gravel, bricks and dirt. Pedestrians try valiantly to navigate the streets. Senior citizens have given up walking. The worst affected are the pushcart fruit vendors who have no option but to share the single lane with honking automobiles. As for the wandering cows, where have they gone?

This hits close to home for me because I fractured my big toe on one of these sidewalks recently.

One moment, I was striding along in my white and red Jamdani saree. The next moment, one of the sidewalk tiles tilted like a garbage-can opener. I fell into the gutter, quite literally.

---

[12]Mahatma Gandhi National Rural Employment Guarantee Act

There was blood and tears. I discovered that my great toe was fractured. A kind orthopedic doctor in the nearby Frazer Town put what is called 'a buddy-bandage', connecting my great toe with my middle toe. I was advised bed rest for two to three weeks. Ten days later, my father passed away.

Although I had visited my ailing father pretty much every single day, I could not go and visit him during the last 10 days of his life. I was lying in bed, keeping my foot raised up. The sequence of events filled me with guilt and regret until a kind friend told me, 'Perhaps your absence was what was needed for your Dad's soul to release itself from the earth. Because when loved ones hang around, the soul does not want to leave.'

It is something that I think about constantly as I pick my way through my beloved city's streets. I don't step on the sidewalk tiles any more. Instead, I gingerly place one foot forward and then another. Muscle memory, they say, lasts longer than other types of memories. This holds true for me. Every step is a test. Will I fall into the gutter or not?

The dug-up streets are particularly galling because this is Bangalore. You see, this city has so much going for it. All the government needs to do is preserve it. The weather is salubrious pretty much all year round. The people are genteel and largely welcoming. There is the infectious start-up energy all around, attracting the young and the curious from all parts of the world. Bangalore is a land of lakes. The trees here were planted by Hyder Ali and Tipu Sultan. There are ancient rock engravings right in Hebbal. Save Maharashtra, this city can hold its own in the sporting element too—we have Rahul Dravid, Anil Kumble, Prakash Padukone and Mahesh Bhupathi. There are wildlife enthusiasts, thanks to the access to the Nilgiri Biosphere nearby. There are conservation scientists like Ullas and Krithi Karanth, and philanthropists like Rohini Nilekani and Azim Premji. This surfeit of riches is perhaps why it is so galling when the politicians take a perfectly lovely city and mess it up.

At the BIC (Bangalore International Centre), which hosts more programmes today than the much older IIC (India International Centre) used to, the citizenry comes together to talk and bemoan their falling, failing city. Activists carrying banners stand outside Town Hall and Freedom Park, trying to effect change.

As for me, I want to join all these protests. For that, I have to get out to my own street, which I currently cannot, because you see—and you know where I am going with this, right?—it is all dug up.

Aiyyo Shraddha ought to do an episode about Bangalore's dug up streets. Perhaps then, the powers that be will pay attention.

Why are Hospital Billing Systems So Bad?

Is it just Bangalore or are hospital billing systems bad all over India?

My aunt suffered a fall and had to be hospitalized. Hairline fracture on her wrist. The orthopedist said that she needed surgery. So here we are, at one of Bangalore's top hospitals—let us call it Mortis—at 7.00 a.m.

Most of us enter hospitals with pain and shame, rage and frustration. In India, we blame the victim. Visiting relatives walk in and say, 'Arrey, why did you fall?' As if it was done on purpose. 'In the future, tell yourself that you will not slip,' they advise.

When enough relatives blame you for your mishap, you start questioning: why me? Why did this happen now? There are no answers, and so we become sad, mad and worried. We enter the hospital with our vulnerabilities exposed. We leave the hospital beaten down, resigned and oddly grateful that we are alive and discharged.

Hospitals, like law enforcement and most government offices, are functioning organizations yet dysfunctional. Over the last few years, thanks to my elders, I have been inside many hospitals. There are many difficult moments for a patient, which is why it makes sense for hospitals to figure out how to make the incoming and outgoing experience for patients pleasant. But they haven't. The admission and billing systems for most hospitals are terrible. Which sucks because, as a patient, you have been feeling the sting of helplessness anyway.

By the time my aunt was wheeled upstairs for surgery, it was 9.00 a.m. The nurses asked her to remove all her jewellery and she hesitated. For women of my mother's generation, removing their jewellery is a disrobement—an act that is imbued with many cultural and familial memories. Whether it is the *mangalasutra* (auspicious thread or necklace), earrings or even the red and green glass bangles, these are only taken off when you become a widow. In the end, they had to put plaster around some of my aunt's toe-rings because they simply wouldn't come out.

One nice thing about Indian doctors is that they chit-chat. They take stock of the patient beyond her illness. This was the case with the anaesthetist and the orthopedic surgeon. We learned that the surgeon's 94-year-old grandmother in Chikkamagaluru had fallen down and broken her hip but the family didn't want her to have surgery.

'Even though you, her grandson, are an orthopedic surgeon?' we asked.

'Well, I am going to drive down there and bring her here for surgery,' he replied. 'There is no other way.'

All went well until discharge time. Which was to be 4.00 p.m. By then, my aunt was hungry and exhausted. She hadn't eaten the whole day. The nurse's station told us that until I went down and paid the bill, they couldn't release her. Fair enough. I went down and the billing said that the OT (Operation Theatre) hadn't released the bill because some of the pins and wires that they had used for the surgery had not been included in the bill. So I went back to the nurse's station and told them to call the OT to find out why. They cleared it. I went back to billing and was told that the purchase department that procured the orthopedic pins still hadn't signed off on them. In case some special pins were used, they needed to check the cost with the supplier. The same with the pharmacy. Which brings me to the crux of this article.

In a city that prides itself on using technology to ease business, why are hospital billing systems so archaic and the opposite of user-friendly? I don't know what system Mortis uses but I have seen the same scrambling happen in all other Bangalore hospitals as well. I don't think it is the fault of any particular individual. In our situation, if the cost of the specialized pins that were used in the surgery had been included in the bill right at the beginning when they were used in the surgery, it would have saved us three hours. But since each department in a hospital is busy all the time and they don't really 'talk' to each other, lots of things fall through the cracks. It is only when patients demand to be discharged and you are standing in the billing department begging to pay the bill so that you can take your patient home that they begin to collect the data about the patient. Why can't this be automated?

A neighbour of mine lost her husband at the hospital. Again, it was the same sorry story. She waited in line, a grief-stricken widow, to pay the bills to take her spouse's body home. Hospitals use phrases like 'patient care' as a marketing tool. Yet, when the time comes, they fail us.

Automating hospital billing systems is the only way to improve the patient experience. It isn't rocket science. Why aren't hospitals doing it?

Where to Shop in Bangalore?

This is one of the most frequent questions that I get asked by visiting friends: where do you shop in Bangalore?

And the answer in the great Indian tradition is 'depends on what you want to buy.'

The problem is that most visitors don't know what they want to buy because they don't know what's available. Most people want choices. They want cute and surprising items that they can use. They want something meaningful that will align with their values, be it buying vegan fair-trade objects or handmade clothes. They want memories. Think of the masks that you brought back from Africa, the Balinese puppets that hang on your wall or the Ganjifa cards that remind you of that amazing trip to Orissa.

Some cities are better shopping destinations than others. If you leave out the triumvirate of London, Paris and Milan, then Istanbul has its Grand Bazaar, New York has Fifth Avenue, Morocco has its souqs and Chennai has Amethyst.

Bangalore, thankfully, has several lovely stores that make browsing and shopping a real treat. Here is a list of a few of my favourite haunts. I have not included chains or franchises such as Good Earth or Forest Essentials in this list; just local stores.

- **Ffolio:** Yashodhara Shroff gave Bangalore its earliest multi-brand boutique. Located at Lavelle Road, Ffolio is a great place to source distinctive Indian designers. In addition, Ffolio invites textile specialists to showcase their work. A recent one was Mumbai's Belaa Sanghvi who brought her Patan Patolas to exhibit at Ffolio.

- **Cinnamon:** This beautifully restored bungalow houses cups, bags and clothes—all curated by Radhika Poddar. Buy stationery, scarfs or Peachoo's beautifully crafted blouses that will uplift every saree. Walk across the street to have a cup of coffee at Maverick & Farmer while you watch young cricketers play.
- **Ambara:** Most people go to Ambara near Ulsoor Lake to buy plants. The Basava Ambara in Basavanagudi is more picturesque. But I have bought well-priced sarees and blouses from this store for years.
- **Raintree:** Take a breath as you step into this bungalow across the street from the ITC Windsor. Parking here is a breeze. The Anokhi store inside provides the anchor, as does Amrapali. Jason Cherian and other South Indian fashion designers showcase their work here.
- **Dwaraka:** This Malleshwaram store stands for Development of Weavers and Rural Artisans in Kalamkari Art. If you like the lovely and ghee-scented original kalamkari work, you should check it out because Anita Reddy is a crusader.
- **Vermilion House:** Owned by textile aficionados Purvi Patel, Bina Rao and Uma Rao, the boutique in Benson Town does exhibitions and conversations about handmade textiles and crafts. Vinay Narkar showcased Dakkani sarees at one such exhibition.
- **Saanchi Antiques & Treasures:** Located in leafy Langford Town with a lovely café on top, Saanchi does high-quality antique furniture and curios. Owned and operated by an old Bangalorean, Parwathi Mirlay, this is the place to go if you want timeless furniture.
- **The House of Angadi:** With boutiques in North and South Bangalore, this Bangalore-brand is a shopping destination that is most beloved for its silk sarees. Designer K.H. Radharaman's restless mind ensures that tradition matches trend. Buy their in-house brand, Alamelu.
- **Chumbak:** Although this is now an all-India brand, it was born in Bangalore.

- **Encrustd:** This label by Bangalore-based Deepa Chikarmane focusses on hand-embroidered and handmade Western wear. Try their shimmery dresses for parties.
- **The Collage Shop:** One of the older boutiques of Bangalore which has now morphed into a crowd-pleaser that caters all things to all kinds of people.
- **House of Taamara:** An Indiranagar boutique that focusses on trendy handwoven sarees and blouses.
- **Cauvery Handicrafts Emporium:** A must-stop if you want to buy Karnataka-specific curios that include sandalwood oil, Mysore sandal soap and local Karnataka crafts.
- **P.N. Rao Fine Suits and Paresh Lamba Signatures:** They are good places to go to if you want tailored menswear.
- **Safina Plaza:** This place has exhibitions that sell everything from speciality *supari* (mouth freshener) to handblocked fabric by the yard. Go here to buy costume jewellery, inexpensive table runners and knick-knacks.
- **Brigade Road and Commercial Street:** These two are great shopping streets. The saying goes, 'Besides your mother and father, you get everything here.' Other good areas for shopping are Avenue Road and Chickpete in the old city but you need to know where to go in these neighborhoods.
- **Government emporium on M.G. Road:** You cannot leave Bangalore without buying a Mysore Silk; and for that, you should head to this spot.
- **Tonique:** It's is a relatively new store which is worth visiting if you want to get a sense of what Bangaloreans drink in terms of wine and spirits.
- **The Hatworks Boulevard:** This retail space houses a lovely set of shops just off busy Cunningham Road. There are pop-ups and crafts markets held here as well.
- **Jayanagar 4th Block shopping complex:** The go-to place for a taste of South Bangalore. It has puja items, costume jewellery and wooden bric-bracs.
- **Blossom Book House and Gangarams Book Bureau:** These

are two places that visiting Bangaloreans check out to buy old and new books.

Sure, Bangalore is not as brand-crazy as Delhi. It may not be as trendy as Mumbai or as traditional as Chennai; but in its acceptance of all things cosmopolitan, this city manages to offer the one thing that every shopper wants: choice.

How to Bargain in Bangalore

The thought occurred as I eyed a stunning silver dinner set in a jewellery store on Commercial Street in Central Bangalore. Plates, tumblers, katoris, the works.

The slight smile on the wizened shopkeeper's face suggested that he was willing to bargain. But where to begin?

Middle age brings many challenges—home, job, mortgage and the realization that you can actually learn something from your parents. So I walked out of the store and called my mother.

'Ma, teach me how to bargain,' I said plaintively.

'My dearest child,' cooed my mother. 'I knew you would see sense.'

When she heard I was contemplating buying silver, she promptly passed the baton to a specialist in this area. 'Call Lily Aunty,' she commanded.

I come from a long line of bargaining women, who can, with one eye, take apart an object and drive the shopkeeper to tears with the other. In spite of this, or perhaps because I have watched them haggle down the price of everything from a teak dining table to a tomato, I have been an awkward and sniffy bargainer—always scolding my mother and aunts for being cheapskates.

In the last few years, I took refuge online—buying Jai Hind pens, Agra *dal moth* snack, Amritsari pickle, Hyderabadi lac bangles, beta-blockers, stinky cheese, equally stinky ayurvedic oils and *neti* pots without speaking to a single human being. Bargaining was so last century, I thought. Then I saw the silver dinner set.

At this large jewellery store that shall remain nameless, people crowded around the counters, buying gold and silver for the 2,000-people weddings that were beginning to happen in Palace Grounds. Lily Aunty, with her penchant for precious metals, would fit right in.

Lily Aunty is from the Konkan coast. She has light green eyes, brown hair and light skin. For decades, the family gossip was that Lily Aunty was half-French. But Lily Aunty had one trait that endeared her to all her jealous sisters-in-law—she was a killer bargainer. It wasn't because of any one thing that she did. It was who she was.

Bargaining, like flirtation, is more attitude than technique, more style than skill. There are no set steps that you can follow. Instead, bargaining is about being playful, irreverent, even sexy—channeling your inner Helen...or Rekha—from *Khoobsurat*, not *Umrao Jaan*. You have to flatter, charm, tease and cajole—all the qualities that had been drummed out of me by years of Covid sheltering-in-place.

So we went, Lily Aunty and I, to hobnob with the wedding shoppers. Fortified by a some hot jalebis from Santhanam Sweets & Savouries down the road, we arrived at one of the most famous names in jewellery in Bangalore.

'Remember, just because he says the silver plate costs ₹10,000 doesn't make it so,' said Lily Aunty with perverse but compelling logic. 'To you, the silver plate may be worth ₹100. To you, a single scoop of *badam* halwa from Asha Sweet Centre in Malleshwaram may be worth more than all the silver in his shop.'

'Or a benne dosai from CTR in Malleshwaram,' I added, feeling more hungry by the minute.

'In other words, it is all a question of perceived value,' chimed in her husband, Rao Uncle, the economics professor, who was the designated driver, or in this case, given how crowded the area was, the designated car 'parker'.

Lily Aunty looked at him like he had sprouted two heads. 'What do men know about these matters?' she said dismissively.

Most men are famously bad bargainers. They don't have the

sense of entitlement of a Gujarati grandmother or the swagger of a Punjabi matron, both of whom can—without wincing—ask for something at a price that will put the merchant out of business.

South Indians like Lily Aunty and my Mom fake ferocity and have a flair for insults—all delivered with a saccharine sweet smile and what I call 'the sexy rowdy approach'—like Rajinikanth. But really, there is no rule book. I know Mathur women who can flirt their way into a good deal. Their Lucknowi counterparts submerge a salesman under an ocean of polite flattery. Uninformed novices like me, on the other hand, gloat when we get a car salesman to knock ₹1,000 off the ₹349,999 sticker price—instead of offering only ₹1,000 for the car, as any self-respecting Indian grandmother would.

'Lily Aunty, go easy,' I said as we entered the store. 'I live in this area. I don't want to be thrown out of the store, or worse, blacklisted by all the shopkeepers of Commercial Street.'

'First rule of bargaining—keep an open mind,' said Aunty sagely. 'The world, my dear, is full of possibilities.'

With that cryptic statement, she sailed into the store in a cloud of imitation Dior perfume, jangling bangles, French chiffon and a homemade pink *potli*-bag.

I shook my head from side-to-side like wrestlers do before a fight. And then I walked into the arena. You won't believe what happened.

Read on...

Hostage negotiators would have a hard time in Bangalore because folks here upend the whole logic with their bargaining. In any negotiation, goes the business saying, you have to create a win–win situation for everyone. That is an anathema to the folks on Avenue Road in Bangalore, whose idea of bargaining is more like a sumo wrestler bringing his opponent to heel. The goal is to pummel the opponent, who in this case, happens to be a hapless shopkeeper.

Do you know how to bargain? For vegetables, clothes, jewels or electronics? If you are under 20, I would wager not. A part of the reason why this generation doesn't have any bargaining skill has to do with the speed of transactions and the way the shopping experience is set up. Either you exclusively shop online, as we all have done in the last few years, or you go to the mall, zip through several stores and pay what they ask. It's fast, efficient and it works. So why waste time haggling?

This particular argument holds no merit for compulsive bargainers like my aunt, Lily. To them, bargaining is not a transaction or a means to an end. It is like drinking Horlicks after doing your homework. It is a way to add sweetness to a chore. The actual money involved is almost besides the point. This was what I found out at a jewellery shop on Commercial Street.

There is a cost, of course. Shopping with Lily Aunty takes four hours longer than usual and usually ends up in a cloud of insults, combined with an ingestion of antacid upon return to the house.

So when I called Lily Aunty to help me buy a beautiful silver dinner set, I imposed a set of rules. She couldn't feign heart attacks. Second, she could not claim to be related to Shilpa Shetty, Aishwarya Rai or Deepika Padukone. She was a Bunt from Mangaluru but that didn't make her a movie star. Third, she had to open negotiations at 50 per cent of the asking price and not five per cent, as is her wont. Fourth, she had to stop cursing in Konkani. This was the best jewellery store in Bangalore, I said, not some Mangaluru fish market where she had cut her bargaining teeth.

Lily Aunty looked wounded at the last phrase. 'What do you know about buying fish, you vegetarian?' she ground out from between clenched teeth. 'It is harder to buy quality fish in Mangalore than it is to buy silver in Bangalore.'

'Aunty, I mean it this time,' I warned just before we entered. "This shop is not some cottage emporium, okay? I don't want them to blacklist me because of how you negotiate.'

'Look how you are standing,' Aunty scolded. 'Like some foreigner.'

It was true. My stance was defensive. I protected my space,

rather than aggressively hogging it. My tone was matter-of-fact rather than truculent, outraged or, ideally, a combination of both. My attitude indicated my willingness to negotiate.

'Negotiation has no place in shopping,' pronounced Aunty. 'Negotiation means compromise. We want to bend them to our will.'

I had unleashed the serpent, I realized. What now?

'Understand one thing,' said Lily Aunty. 'Words are cheap. Particularly in India. People don't say what they mean and nothing is what it seems.'

This I knew from previous experience. When we were wedding shopping for a cousin, Lily Aunty entered a saree store in Chickpete. She ran a practised eye over the silk sarees behind the glass counter, pronounced them to be 'rubbish' and demanded to be taken to the back room where the 'real stuff' was. The weird thing was that the salesmen gave her more respect after her rudeness, brought her soda and *kolbada* and fussed over her like she was B. Saroja Devi or Bharathi Vishnuvardhan.

When I attempted such assertiveness, my statements came out like a croak; and I was asked to take my business elsewhere.

So we walked in. And there was the silver dinner set that I had kept on hold. The shopkeeper took one look at Aunty, squared his shoulders and smiled wanly. He had met a worthy match.

Egged on by her hot breath on my shoulder, I took a deep breath and simulated the light-headed feeling that comes at the tail end of a 16-hour-long intermittent fast.

'Eshtu?' I drawled, flicking a dismissive finger at the sparkling offerings I coveted. 'How much is this set worth?'

'One lakh,' said the shopkeeper without blinking.

Lily Aunty snorted. I glared at her and pretended to laugh derisively, like Kannada superstar Yash does in the movie *Mr and Mrs Ramachari*.

'*Ree* (which is the Kannada equivalent of the Hindi 'Ji'), don't joke, Ree,' I said.

'Would I lie to you, *Akka*?' He had called me his sister. Game on. 'This is an heirloom set. Custom piece. Only one in entire

Bangalore. I would happily give it to you for free but my boss will kill me.'

'And my mother will kill me if I buy it for anything more than ₹30,000,' I said.

'Nanjudeshwara!' he said, throwing up his arms prayerfully. 'How you joke, sister! Do you know what this is? Silver. Not stainless steel.'

I ended up paying ₹70,000 for the set. Lily Aunty insisted that I had overpaid by ₹50,000 but I was jubilant. In my mind, I had found a bargain.

'Go back to Ulsoor market,' said Lily Aunty witheringly. 'Start with vegetables. That is nursery school for bargaining. Then work your way up to silver.'

As we paid, Lily Aunty delivered the final verdict. She stared scornfully at the shopkeeper. 'You made a mistake, my friend,' she said. 'If you had given a good price, this silly girl would have bought a set for 12 people. Instead, now you are only selling her one set.'

With one sentence, Lily Aunty had managed to make both the shopkeeper and me feel bad. Which, I guess, was the point of it all.

NATURE AND WILDLIFE

Exploring Spiders,
Snakes and Frogs

If you are a nature buff, Bangalore is a great place to be in. Its climate allows people to do the one thing that is needed to engage with nature—be outside. When I go to Delhi or Mumbai, I often wish that there was a primer for nature activities or folks I could connect with. Here then is one such primer for Bangalore.

(Disclosure: This essay—which is neither comprehensive nor entirely without bias—has mentions of some friends and acquaintances.)

As an entry point, get on Telegram. Join a group called 'Bangalore Wildlife'. You will find folks with broad and deep expertise there. For example, Shyamal L. is one of India's top contributors to wildlife for Wikipedia. Seshadri K.S. is a frog expert. Sunil Kumar M. is an ant-lover, who also co-authored a book called *On a Trail with Ants: A Handbook of the Ants of Peninsular India* with Ajay Narendra. T. S. Srinivasa knows Sanskrit and also trees. He has written a book called *Discover Garden Climbers*. The Bangalore Butterfly Club has its own group online.

To meet the real '*daads*' or gurus in the nature community, join the long-running nature outing group that meets in Lalbagh on the second Sunday of every month at around 8.00 a.m. If you are lucky, you will meet experts like Dr S. Subramanya and Dr M.B. Krishna who will point out ferns, fungi, figs and flowers, opening up worlds that you didn't know existed. Naturalist and author Karthikeyan Srinivasan comes often. His book *Explore*

Spiders of India tells us everything we need to do about these fascinating arachnids. It was published by Ecoedu, a niche publisher of field guides on Bangalore's (and sometimes India's) creepers, plants, trees, spiders and more.

Lalbagh is a good place for nature folks, as is Koshy's Café. Prem Koshy himself is a snake catcher, who like me is fascinated by these ancient reptiles that are part of the creation myths of pretty much every civilization.

Wildlife isn't a silo, of course. It is also a route to meet some terrific people. Usha Ramaiah, now 80, for instance, was the first woman in Karnataka to scale the Himalayas. She is now a birder. Hayath Mohammed takes amazing macro shots of insects. Sugandhi Gadadhar, who won a National Geographic grant, makes films on bears, otters and rivers with her husband, Rana Belur. Brothers Rohit and Kalyan Verma's web-zine, *Nature in Focus,* has beautifully laid-out visual stories on zombie fungi or bar-headed geese. Nirupa Rao's illustrations of the magnificent trees of the Western Ghats bring them to tenuous life on the pages of her book *Pillars of Life*. Deepa Mohan conducts walks on several days of the week, all of which she announces on Bangalore's WhatsApp communities and social media.

Some in the community expand their interests. Priya Singh, an independent researcher with an expertise in wild canids (wild dogs), has become a moth expert as well. Interesting tangents emerge. Wildlife conservationist Rickey Key has won two Grammy awards. He inhabits the worlds of art, culture, wildlife and music. Arguably one of the best wildlife filmmaking companies in the world, Felis Films, is based here in Bangalore. Its founder, Sandesh Kadur, grew up cycling around South Bangalore. Late photographer Ramki Sreenivasan co-founded the magazine *Conservation India*. If you think you are 'into' conservation, read filmmaker Shekar Dattatri's brilliant article available on www.conservationindia.org called 'New to Conservation?'

India's finest patron of wildlife and conservation, Rohini Nilekani, makes her home here. Quietly and systematically, she has funded an array of ventures, small and large, that touch pretty much every species. Trees, birds, black panthers and water ecosystems seem to resonate with her. To me, philanthropy towards nature is perhaps the most far-reaching and visionary way to spend your money given that climate change is going to be the buzzword for the next century.

One of the things I do is called Bird Podcast. The producer of this podcast, Ulhas Anand, has connections with many aspects of wildlife here in Bangalore, ranging from the North Bangalore Birding Group that I am part of, to the Valley School birding group. Ulhas was named after pioneering conservation biologist and tiger expert, K. Ullas Karanth—different spelling, I know. But it just goes to show how Bangaloreans think. Imagine naming your child after a wildlife expert rather than a run-of-the-mill film star or politician. Today, Dr Karanth's daughter, Krithi, runs the Center for Wildlife Studies (CWS) with its ambitious goal of 'rewilding' India.

There are two qualities that seem to differentiate wildlife folks from the rest. One is a certain self-sufficiency and contentment with the solitude found in nature. The second is a quiet willingness to share. It helps that Bangalore institutes like the Indian Institute of Science (IISc) and the National Centre for Biological Sciences (NCBS) churn out an impressive array of studies and field biologists.

Now that you have the names of people and places in Bangalore wildlife, why not reach out and connect with us the next time you visit this fair city?

The Pleasure of Bangalore's Parks

For being in the centre of the city, Bangalore's Cubbon Park is remarkably deserted during the day. The Page 3 people[13] who populate nearby UB City are absent here. Instead, the park is left to pedestrians, plebeians and proletariats, which is exactly as it should be. Unlike Central Park, Hyde Park, Lodhi Gardens or Tokyo's Shinjuku, Cubbon Park hasn't been overly gentrified—overtaken by stroller-moms in True Religion jeans, joggers in neon tights or bare-chested drummers who jam all evening. Instead, Cubbon Park remains sedate, even somnolent, offering refuge for tired Bangaloreans who want to decompress in anonymity, amidst nature's soothing balm.

I used to visit Cubbon Park three times a week to walk my dog off-leash while my daughter played tennis. Often, I saw the same people. Rarely would I see anyone I knew, something I have come to cherish. Law clerks from the nearby Attara Kacheri walk across, discussing cases and files. Weary men who look like Arthur Miller's Willy Loman, sit in grey pants and beige shirts under the broad canopy of a fading rain tree, making peace with their thoughts. Furtive lovers lurk in the shadows. Boys speaking Bhojpuri climb trees and chase each other. Burkha-clad women clutch toddlers in shimmering frocks. Two dreadlocked men play frisbee. A British man walks two sleek Weimaraners off-leash. Men urinate under the bamboo bushes. Retirees walk by in eye-popping attire—monkey cap, bright red tilak or *namam*,

---

[13]From 'Page 3 culture', referring to celebrity and lifestyle culture depicted through tabloid stories often featured on the third page of Indian newspapers

white *baniyan* (vest), khakhi shorts, mismatched purple socks and chalk-whitened Bata shoes. A drunk autorickshaw driver gives a loud but perfect rendition of 'Mere Naina, Sawan Bhado'. Nobody misses a step but a sporadic group gives him a walking ovation in the end.

Humans are a minority in Cubbon Park though. The place really belongs to the trees, and boy, are they characters. There is this grandmotherly fig tree with stomach-folds, that seems to have compressed itself to spread its canopy to the maximum extent. People sit in park benches under it. Geckos breed in its fold. Fur-balled squirrels run spirals before jumping off its trunk. Eagles rest on top. The whole thing is quite stunning.

An upstart silk cotton tree arches sideways and upwards like a ballet dancer, surrounded by matronly peepul, gulmohar and banyan trees, all shivering and hovering. You can almost see this young tree navigating and negotiating with these matrons to get its place in the sun. Atop its great height, you see Brahminy kites. Keep looking and a heron flies by.

After walking amidst these trees for the three months, I did something that I have never done. I hugged a Laburnum. This *Cassia fistula* is a common sight in Bangalore. Even my building has one. One evening, I wrapped my arms around this tree for six seconds—that's how long it takes for the beneficial oxytocin hormone to release itself and make you feel good, so if you are hugging your spouse, lover, friend, child or pet, make sure you hug for six seconds at least to get the oxytocin kicking in. So I hugged this tree in Cubbon Park. Nobody paid me a second glance. I had the drunk autorickshaw driver to compete with, after all. That was the turning point. Like a drug addict, I wanted more.

I googled 'trees of Cubbon Park' and came across just one worthwhile site that documented the trees, done by naturalist Karthikeyan Srinivasan. Called *Wild Wanderer*, also known *Karthik's' Journal*, this website documents the flowering trees of Bangalore. I cold-emailed Karthik and asked him if I could walk with him the next time he was in Cubbon Park, which was how I found myself with the 'wild wanderer'.

'Trees as a group can do amazing things,' says Karthik. 'We don't notice because they operate in a different timeline than we humans do.' When I ask for an example, he asks back, 'Have you ever seen a fig flower?' I say 'No.'

'Then how do we get the seed?'

He talks about the enclosed fig inflorescence and the tiny fig wasp, who have been in a co-evolutional relationship for the last 80 million years.

Karthik points to an *Albizia lebbeck* or woman's tongue tree, called so because the rattling of its pods sounds like women chattering. There are the *Java cassias* and the drooping *Millingtonia hortensis* or cork trees. The bauhinias are blooming pink and the sausage tree is shedding thick flowers. A desi badam or *Terminalia catappa* stands, slim and strong, like a teenage girl, preening before guests.

Karthik spent 45 minutes identifying trees in Cubbon Park, but the high point was when I asked about a native Pongam tree. He held its warped, discoloured leaf and said softly, 'Lovely.' Turns out that there were two jumping spiders in the leaves and off he went into an explanation about their mating ritual.

The true gift of spending time with a naturalist is not the species that he identifies, although that is a highlight. The true gift is how naturalists quietly transmit their enthusiasm for nature. Karthik has the kind limpid eyes of a musician who operates in a different dimension. He notices different things than perhaps you and I. He thinks, for instance, that 'arachnids are quite amazing'. When I asked him to repeat the sentence in plain English, he said, 'You know, most of us take a vacation to experience nature—we go on wildlife safaris and such. Nothing wrong with that. But nature surrounds us every day. Every urban Indian is exposed to bees, bugs and spiders. Why not observe and enjoy them? Why give up those pleasures?'

Here is the takeaway: next time you or your kids see a spider, ladybug or even a cockroach, try not to squeal. Instead, become still and observe it. You won't regret it. Oh, and consider hugging a tree. Like a pet who will listen to you sob your broken heart out, without any seeming reaction, these trees will make you feel better. I know this because I was a sceptic converted into a regular tree-hugger. Just like Prem Koshy (of Koshy's in Bangalore) and others like him.

Bangalore, by the way, is full of tree-huggers. It is one of the best things about this city.

NEIGHBOURHOODS

Bangalore Neighbourhoods: V.V. Puram

My mother's theory about kesari bhaath, the sweet dish that defines Karnataka cuisine, is that it ought to have enough ghee to slide down your throat with nary a chew or swallow. I thought about this as I stood outside Chandra Chat Centre in Vishveshwara Puram or V.V. Puram, a bustling neighbourhood in Basavanagudi, South Bangalore.

I once wanted to live here, because Basavanagudi, along with Malleshwaram, gave us the portmanteau word for R.K. Narayan's fictional town—Malgudi. I went to Thindi Bheedhi (literally 'tiffin street'), V.V. Puram's 'khau galli', which is to Bangalore what Chandni Chowk's food streets are to Delhi. It was around 6.00 p.m., just when the area was opening up for the evening's business. I went there because I was suffering from post-Diwali food-withdrawal symptoms. I decided that instead of fasting or going on diets and detoxing like my sensible friends, I would simply eat some more.

Where to begin, that was the question. S. Ravindra, a friend of mine who lives in Basavanagudi, said that one cannot get a bad vada in Bangalore. What does this mean for a visitor? If someone takes you to a darshini (similar to dhaba), opt for a vada in some form—either dunked in sambhar or rasam or with chutney—and you won't go wrong.

In V.V. Puram, one of the vadas on offer is made with the hyacinth bean or avarekai. It is seasonal and local—two words that chefs all over the world love. Avarekai, along with kadlekai (peanuts), are beloved to Bangaloreans. In fact, V.V. Puram hosts the annual avarekai mela in winter (December–January). A variety of dishes are made from both the peeled and the unpeeled bean. By some estimates, some 1,000 kg of this bean gets traded everyday at the mela.[14]

I was with Kunal Bysani whose Instagram handle, Ghatotkatcha, explains his love of food. A fifth-generation Bangalorean, Kunal, was there to give me a tour of the places he likes in Thindi Bheedhi.

We begin with V.B. Bakery (or Vishveshwarapuram Brahmins Bakery) known for its khara biscuits, rusk and *dumrot*. Dumrot comes individually packed and resembles a pockmarked creme brulee, except it has shredded ashgourd (*petha* or *kumblekai*) mixed with dense amounts of ghee. Since I am a savoury person, I opt for the KBC or Khara Bun Congress.

Congress peanuts is what Bangalore calls masala peanuts. Reason: these peanuts are cleaved in half, much like the Congress Party was in 1969. The KBC is a bun cut in half, generously smeared with butter and filled with Congress peanuts. Or maybe this snack was popular in Congress party meetings. Whatever the reason, Congress peanuts are available all over Bangalore.

A weird change happened to me after I moved to Bangalore. I have come to prefer idlis over dosas. Bangalore does idli well. There are rava idlis—invented in MTR, Bidadi's *thatte* idli which is about the size of a small plate, and of course, the normal idlis. I had both the thatte idlis and the normal ones in Thindi Bheedhi and they were outstanding.

Where do you eat this? Sai Idli Mane or Sri Gurudeva Eating House, it doesn't matter. They are all excellent. Go where the crowds are and you won't go wrong.

If North Indian is your preference, go to Dev Sagar, which serves excellent *dabeli*—although I hesitate to say this, given that

---

[14]Ranganna, Akhila, 'In Bengaluru, an Ode to Broad Beans at the Avarekai Mela', *Indian Express*, 18 January 2016, https://tinyurl.com/m9a344dz. Accessed on 19 June 2023.

I am not a North Indian and have no notion of what constitutes an excellent dabeli. I guess you Mumbaikars or Delhiwallas have to try these out to make sure.

At the end of Thindi Bheedhi are the vendors on pushcarts. A man called 'Ashok Uncle' purveys corn in a variety of ways. You can get baby corn masala chat, which is basically sliced baby corn with mango and spices. The *bhutta* or roasted corn is terrific here. Kunal says that Ashok churns out 'sustainable food before sustainability became a watchword.' The baby corn chat, for instance, is given to me in the corn peels. Leftovers are parcelled in reusable mixture covers. There is no trash around the shop.

Next door is Shivanna Gulkand Centre. Here, fresh *gulkand* (preserve made from fresh rose petals and sugar) becomes the base for ice cream and fruits that become more and more elaborate. Mine had chocolate covered almonds strewn on top. What I would do the next time is just try plain gulkand which tastes fresh without being cloying.

After a night of eating, try the masala soda at Sri Ganesh Fruit Juice Centre. The owner will pour you a masala soda and the deal is that you have to continuously keep sipping as he pours till the bottle is empty. This is a 'bottoms up' tango between the pourer and the drinker. At the end, those who succeed get rewarded with a 'good boy' or 'good girl'.

Next time, I will go back and try the dosas. There is masala dosa, akki dosa, ragi-millet dosa and many more.

Bangalore Neighbourhoods: Shivaji Nagar

We each have our post-Covid resolutions. One of mine is to walk, not on a treadmill or inside a gated community, but out on the streets. To be able to walk in and through crowded thoroughfares, and that too, without a mask, is a gift.

Much like any other global city, Bangalore is also composed of neighbourhoods, each with its own unique charm. I live in the Shivaji Nagar area that was called 'Black-Palli' earlier. There are many reasons for this. Some say it was named by the British because 'black' Indian folks used to worship at a *palli* or church here. The church in question is St Mary's Basilica in the centre of Shivaji Nagar. Historian S.K. Aruni says that the area may have been named after John Blakiston, who designed the Bangalore Cantonment. Another story is more fanciful. It says that the name came from *bili akki palli* which means 'white rice area'. The packed streets in Shivaji Nagar make it hard to imagine rice fields being here. An Urdu-medium school called GUHPS Black Palli bears witness to this colonial past.

Mornings are quiet in Shivaji Nagar and you can walk through the streets, picking up fresh vegetables, fish, meat or whatever it is you fancy. Here is my incomplete and individual list of offerings from this neighbourhood.

- Have a vada curry or a pulao with onion raita at BN Sambaiah Setty Tiffin Room, a tiny hotel packed with morning regulars who come here for breakfast.

- Take a walk to the Sree Ekambareshwara Dharamraja Temple at the end of Dharmaraja Koil Street, buying fresh flowers, fruits and vegetables along the way. The best time for a walk is at 7.30 a.m. when there are no crowds.
- Walk further down to Russell Market. Duck in to watch fragrant tuberose being strung into garlands, meat being butchered and vegetables being unpacked for the day's business.
- Have a cutting chai and rusk at New Bilal Tea Centre or at any of the tiny tea stalls around Russell Market.
- As the sun comes up, walk into any of the textile stores on Seppings Road for fabrics that you can get tailored as you please. Sri Dhanalakshmi Stores is an old favourite, as are Balu, Varalakshmi and Sri Ganesh.
- If glitzy sequined fabric is what you are after, step into the crowded Evening Bazar, Femina Bridal Collection or Pakeeza Collection, also on Seppings Road.
- Visit any of the temples that pay homage to the fierce tribal goddesses who rule this area. Ask for the nearest Om Shakthi temple. Other names are Muthyalamma, Angala Parameshwari, Amman or Nagamma. If you are lucky, there will be *pallaki* or chariot festival, called 'Car Festival' in this area, where the goddess is taken out in a procession with drum beats, dancing and donations. This only happens in the evenings though.
- In the evening, drop in at Santhanam Sweets & Savouries for South Indian snacks such as kodubale, chakli, *adirasam* and *namkeen* mixture similar to what Gujaratis call *farsan*.
- Round the corner from Santhanam, on Veerapillai Street are two local favourites—Naveen Butter Dosa Camp and Shree Idly Corner, both excellent. End your meal with a *milk-khova* from Priya Milk Kova Dairy.
- Ask about Sri Ramula Sannidhi temple on Sri Ramulu Sannidhi Street. Across the temple, just outside what looks

174 ■ Namma Bangalore

like a home, is a man selling piping hot kuzhi paniyarams. Only available in the evenings and at around 8.30 a.m. in the morning.

- At the corner of Ibrahim Sahib Street and Jeweller's Street and beside LMR Jewellers is K. Raju Jewellers—a place generations of college girls have gone to have their ears, noses, belly buttons and other organs of the body pierced. Both my daughters have been going to Raju for years. He scolds them that they have too many ear-piercings, even though that is his business.

- Walk down Ibrahim Sahib Street to Silver Palace. An old-fashioned *achari* or jeweller sits in the lane beside Silver Palace. He can repair your broken gold ornaments and fashion new ones, all out of a tiny shop. Go further down this lane to the end and you will find a catering business run by two women. They sell lemon sevai—₹250 for a kilo but you have to come with a vessel and pick it up.

- Visit Marudhar Papers on Lubbay Masjid Street, if you love stationery. There are several paper agencies in the area such as Padam Paper & Stationery, Varsha Gift & Stationery and Fine Paper World. Here, I once chose thick Italian paper, perfect for my fountain pen. I had them cut down to a custom size that would fit into the orange Hermes pocket diary that I carry in my handbag. Talk about mixing extremes—the local with the global.

- Also in Lubbay Masjid Street, in Puttur House, is a place I have wanted to visit, but haven't. These are traditional bonesetters who will massage a broken bone and set it in the right place.

- On nearby Jumma Masjid Road, you can find sequined Indian *juttis* (traidtional slip-on footwear), *chikankari* fabric and attar. Go here only if you can stand crowds.

- Beside Russell Market on M.F. Noronha Street is J Siddiqi Corner Shop where I have been going to buy flasks, copper jugs and stainless steel vessels for years. This is where I recently bought my cast iron tawa for ₹1,100.

- Behind J Siddiqi are the bamboo basket sellers. Go to Cane Centre on Meenakshi Kovil Street to find bamboo planters, baskets, lamps and even bamboo blinds.
- Walk around and read the street names. They are Hindu, Muslim and Christian, referencing a syncretic India where Hindus go and pray to St Mary during the annual St Mary's feast that happens in September, Christians buy puja products and everyone realizes that the best shops will be closed on Friday afternoons during Namaz or prayer time.

This is India.

Street Art in Malleshwaram

Art holds a dubious place in many circles. There are those who self-righteously say, 'I just don't understand this modern art.' There are economists and investors who put a price tag on this deep human instinct to paint and express—just go to the Bhimbetka caves in Madhya Pradesh to see early rock art. There is the art that is taught in schools. As children get older, art gets taken out in lieu of maths and science. Globally, art departments suffered a lot of funding-cuts, thanks to the pandemic. And then there is art that is inclusive, expansive and out on the streets. Never before did we make art more than during the pandemic when were all stuck at home.

You want proof? Come to Malleshwaram in Bangalore and you will see a colourful, spirited and resounding defense to the question: of what value is art?

It was art that drew me to Malleshwaram many a time during Covid. Walking through Malleshwaram's streets where artists have painted an ode to their neighbourhood is a joyous and healing experience. But let's begin at the beginning.

In early April of 2021, a group of artists got together to paint the walls in different parts of Malleshwaram (and indeed all through Bangalore). There is Anpu Varkey's mural of the white-saree clad feet of a woman near Seva Sadan. Round the corner in a tiny lane, Chandana B.V. has painted the champaka or sampige flowers that fill Malleshwaram with their scent. Diagonally across the road is a mural of a woman contemplating a fresh cup of filter coffee—by artist Enoch Dheeraj Ebenezar. Artist Girija Hariharan has painted a lovely portrait of saree-clad women surrounded by marigolds in the lane just behind Veena Stores, known for its idlis. Spandana Vella has painted sparrows, beloved to Bangaloreans. Saksham Verma has created the title, Malleshwaram, in many hues—in English and Kannada. There are other artists who came together to form Geechugalu, a collective that has painted these murals.

You can see their murals throughout Bangalore on their website which can be accessed at www.geechugalu.wordpress. com. Or you can go to the Facebook page of 'Geechugalu' or 'Bengaluru Moving' to see their work with its up-to-the-minute hashtag, #malleshwaramhogona or 'let's go to Malleshwaram'. As my dancer friend, Madhu Natraj, says, 'Do you need any more proof that Malleshwaram is the centre of the universe?'

But then, I knew that, Madhu.

It was art that took me to Malleshwaram. What is interesting though, is the foundation upon which all this art flowered. A number of civic and government agencies have joined hands with passionate private citizens to create these murals and street art.

Take Bengaluru Moving for instance. It promotes a cause that is dear to all Indians—safe streets for walking. Bangalore's traffic is horrendous. We all agree on that, even those who love this city. The way forward is public transport, like Namma Metro and pedestrian-friendly streets. The goal is to encourage more citizens to use 'non-motorized transport' like bicycles or our own two feet. But how does one walk in a city that is all dug up?

Enter the lanes that architect Suchitra Deep calls 'conservancies'. Suchitra (and let me use her given name instead of the journalistic last name version please) lives and works in Malleshwaram. As we walk together through the congested thoroughfares of Malleshwaram, Suchitra quickly turns into tiny lanes that run parallel to the main streets. These, she says, are conservancies that were used primarily for manual scavenging when Malleshwaram used to have large leafy plots with multi-family bungalows. Today, these tiny lanes have no traffic and are a pleasure to walk through.

In fact, I couldn't believe that they were right in the heart of the city. No horns, no scooters—just me and the art that lined the walls. Very civilized, very healing.

Suchitra has been mapping the conservancies since 2013. A confluence of grants kick-started her budding idea to convert them into walking streets. The community group she is part of, Malleswaram Social, collaborated with Sensing Local which is an 'urban-living lab', according to its website. Sensing Local works on a variety of issues to help create sustainable cities. Together, they created M-ULL (Malleshwaram Urban Living Lab) and won a grant from the Department of Urban Land Transport (DULT) as part of its Sustainable Urban Mobility Programme (SuMA). Sensing Local also got other grants with the goal of improving pedestrian-friendly streets. These grants brought in artists. So there you go: a government department (DULT) helped a variety of urban initiatives to beautify streets.

What is Suchitra's learning from all this? 'I had many ideas as an architect but my own limitations stopped me from going further. Each collaborator we brought on board gave us more reach but still we needed funds. DULT stepping in helped us with that and involved the government. The Purpose grant helped bring in the artists. The moment you have artwork on this scale, it makes it pop. So, it takes the coming together of many individuals and organizations to make change happen in the correct way.'

Take a walk through Malleshwaram and see for yourself what she is talking about.

THINGS TO DO

36 Things to Do in Bangalore

A very specific Bangalorean take.

1. Go into Cauvery Handicrafts Emporium at the corner of M.G. Road and Church Street to buy some sandalwood oil.
2. Walk down Church Street without worrying about jostling around with the other million people that are there.
3. Go to Koshy's and sit for hours shooting the breeze with the folks who have been coming here for decades—including naturalist Krishna M.B., publisher Ramjee Chandran, singer Radha Thomas, actress Kirtana Kumar, historian Ramachandra Guha and the owner, Prem Koshy.
4. Walk down the road to Blossom Book House and Gangaram Book Bureau to browse through the latest books. Pick up a few.
5. Accompany a friend to Empire Restaurant at the end of Church Street at 2.00 a.m. for their chicken. I, as a vegetarian, can only smell the stuff.
6. Run through Cubbon Park at dawn and smile at the other runners.
7. Go to The Ritz-Carlton spa for their heavenly aroma massages.
8. Have a North Indian meal at The Royal Afghan in ITC Windsor. Have double servings of the the dal bukhara and their *kulchas*.
9. Go to Vidyarthi Bhavan for breakfast. Have a rava vada and a masala dosa.
10. Have a benne dosa along with a Mangalore bajji at CTR, now called Sri Sagar Hotel.

11. Visit Natya Institute of Kathak and Choreography in Malleshwaram to watch a rehearsal in progress in their studio. Walk downstairs to the Craft Council shop, Kamalini, and buy handmade bags, puppets and trays.
12. Walk down Gandhi Bazaar and bargain freely with the street vendors for fresh vegetables.
13. Taste the freshest fruits at the markets of Malleshwaram.
14. Go to K.R. Market at 8.00 a.m. and smell the fragrant mallige or jasmine that arrives in bulk to be sold to Bangalore's flower vendors who fan out all over the city with fragrant strings of jasmine, champaka, *tulsi* and *davanam*.
15. Stand in line outside Food Camp in Malleshwaram for their Sunday lunch.
16. Spend a couple of hours at Angadi Silks in Jayanagar. Pick up a silk saree or two from their latest collection.
17. Go with friends to Byg Brewski Bewing Company in Hennur and sample their offerings. If you live on the other end of Bangalore, go to Red Rhino, The Bier Library or Windmills Craftworks.
18. Catch a Kannada play at Ranga Shankara or Jagriti theatres.
19. Go to Lalbagh on the weekends for specialized walks offered by Ecoedu. Look for the walk about the creepers of Lalbagh.
20. Take an early morning motorcycle ride with Harley Davidson India riding club. Go to Nandi Hills with them for breakfast. Then work off the calories by climbing Nandi Hills.
21. On the way back, stop at the Four Seasons Hotel for a champagne lunch.
22. Go to the BIC on any evening for scintillating panel discussions and company. Have a bite at their in-house restaurant after.
23. Visit any of the hoary old places of worship, and Bangalore has many. Holy Trinity Church or Infant Jesus Church. The Bull Temple or Sri Someshwara Swami Temple. The Jain temples of Ulsoor. The big mosque, Masjid e Khadria, at the end of Nandi Durga Road.

24. Visit The Mythic Society in Chamarajpet for rare books and great atmosphere.
25. Sit with the music lovers of Bangalore either at Gayana Samaj in Basavanagudi or Chowdiah Memorial Hall in Malleshwaram. Wait for the Ramaseva Mandali concerts and nod en masse to Carnatic music.
26. Take a Vayu Vajra green bus to the airport. Have tea at Chai Point before boarding the flight.
27. Have breakfast at The Oberoi. Sit in its garden and savour their omelettes.
28. Go to any of Bangalore's lakes for birdwatching—Jakkur Lake, Saul Kere, Hebbal Lake or Hesarghatta Lake.
29. Drive out to SOUKYA for a consultation with Dr Issac Mathai, followed by a customized ayurvedic treatment.
30. Book a corner room at Conrad and enjoy the views of Ulsoor Lake.
31. Go the NGMA on a weekday to enjoy the art without the crowds.
32. Walk down Lavelle Road and duck into any of the shops there. End your walk with a coffee or a swim at Bangalore Club.
33. Visit the Museum of Art and Photography (MAP) and ask for a tour. Walk across the road to the Venkatappa Art Gallery (VAG).
34. Have a pizza at Brik Oven on Church Street or at Sunnys. While you are at Sunnys, try their baked brie or any dessert on the menu.
35. Go to Lupa on M.G. Road to experience Chef Manu Chandra's take on modern cuisine.
36. Hug someone and don't let go.

Creative Ways to Celebrate a Holiday

Every year, the same questions: what are you doing for New Year's? Any plans? Any resolutions? As for resolutions, just say, 'I don't make them, I keep them.'

Here are some suggestions from interesting Bangaloreans about celebrations.

- **Julie Kagti, textile artist:** 'My suggestion would be a quiet sit-down seven-course dinner at Grasshopper, located in a family-run farm on Bannerghatta Road. A few good friends and family, where the wine and conversation flow easy. End with a nightcap by a bonfire, recapping the highlights of the year late into the night.'
- **Ravichander, honorary director BIC:** 'This New Year, I would recommend that you discover our erstwhile city centre on foot. A civilized society cares for its most vulnerable, and that would be the pedestrian on our streets. With our newly-built footpaths, you could, for instance, explore getting from Ulsoor Lake to Freedom Park and back. And there are a myriad of alternative routes on foot where you can cover places, community spaces and food joints. You will discover the Bangalore that you missed experiencing all these years.'
- **Praveen Kumar, Bharatanatyam dancer, guru and founder of Chithkala School of Dance:** 'Being a classical dancer, my life mostly revolves around art, travel and meeting people. I have been associated with the Sri Swanandashrama, which is

off Kanakapura Road, wherein we help kids studying in and around that place. We help them in getting funds to pay their school fee, uniforms etc. So I like to spend the day in that area just to keep a tab on their activities. Also, the Ashram has beautiful greenery, which reminds me of beautiful old Bangalore.'

- **Ruma Singh, wine writer and columnist:** 'If the pandemic has taught us anything it is that we have got a second chance at life. So, it will be a quiet getaway with my family to one of the many beautiful, green places we have around Bangalore like Flameback, surrounded by paddy fields and bird sounds; or Primrose Villas, atop the mist-wrapped mountains of the Western Ghats—both in Chikkamagaluru. I would sit and watch the trees, listen to the birds and immerse myself in the beauty of nature and the present—that joy never gets old. Oh, and a glass of wine to aid the meditation—perhaps a 2013 Alvaro Palacios L'Ermita Velles Vinyes from Priorat.'
- **Abhishek Poddar, founder of the MAP:** 'I realize the true extent of how much I enjoy Bangalore each time I land back in the city. From the smoothest airport in the country 10 minutes from landing to being in the car, the steaming hot cup of filter coffee from Hatti Kaapi in hand, driving back home with the windows down and enjoying the amazing weather. The next morning is always a refreshing walk in the park amongst the flowering trees (and each season has its own colours), followed by the finest South Indian breakfast at Umesh Point! There is no other place that offers so many of life's simple pleasures so amply.'
- **Madhu Natraj, award-winning choreographer, mentor and artpreneur:** 'If I were to imagine a New Year's Eve that is special, I would choose to nominate the majestic stairs and patio of the Vidhana Soudha as a concert venue on 31 December. A unique amalgam of folk, classical and contemporary performers of Karnataka along with an international troupe. The area around Vidhana Soudha could

be cordoned off for a 1-km radius to feature bespoke cuisine and beverages (with local breweries and wineries). This should be a ticketed event with security. If the government—in liaison with event companies and artistes—hosts such an event every year, we don't need to hear of revellers roaming the streets like headless chickens with no idea as to how to spend this special evening.'

- **Madhav Sehgal, general manager, The Leela Palace, Bangalore:** 'My New Year plan is to take a ride on my Harley and visit a few temples in and around Bangalore and find some authentic temple food in their vicinity.'

What would *I* do? Staycations are in. Watching the moonrise and the sunrise from a penthouse suite at Conrad, overlooking Ulsoor Lake, will be a treat.

How to Celebrate Valentine's Day

What is the most flamboyantly romantic gesture that anyone has done for you? Was it a surprise? What if your lover or boyfriend shows up at your birthday or at a friend's wedding—like Ranbir Kapoor did while singing 'Badtameez Dil'?

Or was it an Instagram-worthy proposal in some remote drone-friendly location? That seems to be de rigueur these days.

Historically, Indian romantic gestures used to be softer. Remember two flowers arching towards each other in old Hindi movies?

India as a civilization was steeped in sensuality. Love in ancient India was an act, a metaphor, a symbol and part of our founding myths.

Why am I saying this? Well, there are 96 words for love in Sanskrit, 80 in ancient Persian, three in Greek and only one in English—and that too is a four-letter word.

So, I thought when we must celebrate the patron saint of bees, epilepsy and nowadays romantic love—I mean St Valentine, of course—let's do so in some cool and authentically Indian ways.

I begin by reading a terrific book, *Erotic Poems from the Sanskrit: An Anthology*, by R. Parthasarathy. Available at Blossom in Bangalore, this anthology contains poems that are shockingly specific and open about love and lust.

Consider this poem by Magha, a seventh-century poet in present-day Gujarat.

You can hide her fingernail marks with your shawl
hide with your hand the lip she has bitten
but can you hide her scent that blows
in every direction, shouting out your adultery.[15]

Our ancestors, it seems, were far more licentious, flamboyant, sexual and open than we give them credit for. Go to Khajuraho this year and see for yourself.

Khajuraho is forever linked with Odissi dance, and that got me thinking about the romantic gestures that have been codified in the Natya Shastra. Lovers emote in India. We speak, of course, but we also use gestures to great effect. Consider two very common ones. Creeping up behind a loved one and shutting their eyes with your palms. You see this in paintings, dance and we practise this in real life. Consider the other gesture—touching your fingers to your ears while your eyes plead forgiveness. This, too, is distinctly Indian. Then there is the huffy, mock-angry hair toss—Indian women use their long hair to great effect. This works much better when the hair is braided. What are some personal gestures that you use to flirt with your lover?

Today's romantic gestures aren't so much cultural as they are commercial—candles, roses, greeting cards, heart-shaped balloons, the colour red and chocolate.

With this preamble, here are some Bangalorean suggestions for Valentine's Day:

- Visit the Bangalore flower market at dawn and drench your sweetie in armloads of fresh champaka. It smells of longing, lust and langour.
- Visit one of the many ancient shrines—temples, churches or dargahs—dotting the city and pray for the well-being of your loved ones. As a Hindu, a recent find is the seventeenth-

---

[15]Parthasarathy, R., *Erotic Poems from the Sanskrit: An Anthology*, Colombia University Press, 2017.

century Kadu Malleshwara Temple in the locality that bears its name. But you could also light a candle at the Infant Jesus Church or pray at one of the many mosques in the Benson Town or Shivajinagar area.

- Buy some freshly-flown Dilli paneer at Infinitea on Cunningham Road. Then, return home and make a finger-licking good paneer butter masala. Lick it off each other's fingers. While at Infinitea, try their special teas as well.
- Take the animal you love the most to The Pet People Café and enjoy chef Abhijit Saha's vegan menu with your dog, cat or turtle.
- Enjoy pour-over coffee or a glass of wine at Trippy Goat. Walk down the road to the NGMA to view some art.
- Take your date to Copitas at Four Seasons. The folks at '30 Best Bars' have deemed this as the 'best hotel bar' in India two years in a row. The cocktails are delicious, as are the stunning views.
- Go to Podi & Spice at the BIC with your gang of friends. Try the ghee idlis and the appams here. Located inside the BIC, this well-priced restaurant, helmed by women, has tasty largely-Karnataka cuisine. Buy your drinks from the Arbor Brewing Company that is in-house and have dinner after a BIC talk.
- Buy a Khunn (or Khann) woven dupatta from KaleNele, which focusses on handcrafted treasures of Karnataka. Choose one with fine *kasuti* embroidery. Buy a Chaduranga Chikki Ilkal saree for your Mom while you are at it.
- Walk hand-in-hand down Church Street and do the 'usual' Bangalorean round of Blossom, Gangaram's and Koshy's.
- Jog through Cubbon Park and end it with a perfect Bangalore breakfast at Airlines Hotel.
- Do like the Japanese do. Watch the moon. Go forest-bathing. In this day and age, simply sitting near your lover and holding hands—without having to sanitize them—is a luxury itself.

PEOPLE AND PLACES

Is There Moral Policing in Bangalore?

Do you want to know what the sad thing is? The whole thing was done for 'likes'.

The only way that this particular moral policing story is different from the countless others that are sprouting up all over India is that it is a social media phenomenon. In case you didn't know about this viral video, it happened on a Friday, on 17 September 2021.

In the video, two men stop a Hindu man (identified as such by the red *tilak* on his forehead, visible underneath the helmet he is wearing), and his Muslim woman colleague, wearing a burqa. They ask the Muslim woman why she is travelling with a non-Muslim. They abuse and threaten the two, even as the woman tries to explain that her colleague is merely giving her a lift home. In between, they slap the man, call the woman's husband and abuse him as well. They force the woman to get off the bike and put her in an autorickshaw. You can see the whole sorry scene play out on many television channels.

The weird twist? The accused—the perpetrators of the attack—filmed and posted the video of them doing the act themselves. In other words, the accused publicized their attack.

And I thought such things couldn't happen in a cosmopolitan and progressive city like Bangalore. This happens in Mangaluru where communal tensions are rife, said my journalist friend, but generally not in Bangalore.

The two accused were arrested quickly, something that Kamal

Pant, the then comissioner of Bangalore Police, declared proudly on Twitter. 'Acting swiftly, @BlrCityPolice has identified and secured two accused persons for assault on a bike rider traveling along with a woman of a different faith. A case is registered and firm legal action is initiated.'

Not to be outdone, Basavaraj Bommai, the then chief minister of Karnataka, got on the bandwagon and said that such miscreants would not be tolerated by his administration.

The surprise was the defence. The two youths, Suhail and Nayaz, said that they had posted many such videos in the past and got appreciation for their 'work.' They thought that they would get applause, not an arrest for this escapade too. They told the police that they expected to be lauded for their actions. Ah, the irony—it was done for social media and they were caught by posting on social media.

When I moved to Bangalore in 2005, there were some things about its culture that I took for granted. Good weather was a given, as were the drooping rain trees. It was a cosmopolitan, progressive city where women went to pubs and pensioners rode on bicycles down M.G. Road. While there were enclaves, the Basavangudi Brahmins, Christians in Cooke Town and Muslims in Benson Town came together in places such as Koshy's, MTR or M.M. Road during Ramadan.

The difference today is social media which does three things. It holds a mirror to what is happening around us. It accelerates extremes—both the positive and the negative. And it allows for anonymity or at least it gives that false sense of security. When we troll on Twitter, we expect that nobody will find us out. We don't know that there are ways to harvest data and identities, even if we attack and abuse using false names. This is what happened to the two attackers. Although you don't see their faces, you hear their voices. Plus, they bragged about their 'work' on their social media channels.

The second is the reaction. When a sentiment becomes a hashtag such as #gharwapsi, the encapsulated idea stirs up emotions and a sense of collective angst. This is what happened with #lovejihad and the selective outrage it invoked. The question is: how real is the religious polarization that is supposedly happening in India?

The answer is as nuanced and multi-layered as this great country itself. While all of us were in a froth about the moral policing that was evident in the video of these goons, the real story is that at the end of the day, we witnessed one inescapable fact. Actually, several facts nested inside the main story. And each of these small facts gives us hope for India. Let me present them.

A man gave his female colleague a lift home. He was Hindu, she was Muslim. She was married. He had been giving her a lift home for many days. Her husband knew this. She wore a burqa. He wore a tilak. They were comfortable in their respective faiths. They were also comfortable mingling with people of other genders and faiths. Each of these sentences offers hope. The greatest hope of all—this continues to happen in Bangalore and Meerut, even though moral policing has become a hashtag.

A while ago, the company Manyavar and actress Alia Bhatt were trolled because of an advertisement in which Bhatt, playing a Hindu bride, talked about updating the tradition of *kanyadaan* (the ritual of giving away a daughter in marriage) to *kanyamaan* (giving respect to the daughter). Immediately, outraged Twitter trolls rained abuse on the ad, the company and the actress. Many of them said that they would boycott Manyavar, although how many actually followed through is doubtful. Certainly, Tanishq's revenues remain healthy even though the company found itself in the middle of a similar controversy sometime back.

I, for now, remain hopeful. I believe that India is too vast, heterogenous and multi-layered a country to fit into a Twitter troll's suffocating label. You can generate as much outrage as you want online. You can brag about morals on social media. But at the end of the day, a Hindu male is still going to offer his married female Muslim colleague a lift. For that, I say, thank God—this is still India.

About Shivarama Karanth:
A Giant in Karnataka

Growing Up Karanth, which came out in October 2021, is a biography of Kota Shivarama Karanth, the polymath who has been a towering figure in fiction, drama, *Yakshagana* (ancient theatre form from Karnataka and Kerala) ballets, science encyclopaedias, children's books and much more. Written by Karanth's three children—Ullas, Malavika and Kshama, *Growing Up Karanth* is a wonderful read. (Disclosure: Ullas and his daughter, Krithi, are friends of mine.)

Why do we read a biography? Often, because we want to get to know greatness. We are drawn to charismatic compelling figures and we want to know the 'real person' behind the public persona. *Growing Up Karanth* delivers this in full measure. It takes us inside the life and mind of the Karanth family. It shows us how they lived, the kinds of food they ate, the animals they kept and the connections they fostered.

There are lovely snippets of Shivarama Karanth, the father, whom the children call 'Tata'. Each of them recounts unique episodes. The eldest, Malavika, talks about going with Karanth to meet his friends in the evenings and chatting him up on these long walks. All three children talk about such perambulations with their father, the road trips they took and how he taught them about art, architecture, music and life.

The setting for all this action is Balavana, their family homestead where people would drop in to chat and connect. Here, Karanth held court, wrote his many works of literature, took in students, friends and strays, taught them things and reframed Yakshagana into a modern form while retaining its essence. It is clear that Shivarama Karanth was someone who followed his bliss, whether it was taking on projects that threw the family more into debt or going on a voyage to Europe to see its museums.

It is also clear that his wife, Leela Alva Karanth, was the anchor to his sails. She is portrayed as a vibrant, compassionate and impactful woman, at least in the early years. There are many episodes that portray Leela as someone who goes out of her way to make people comfortable—perhaps, to her detriment, as her later years show. She made conversation with all the important people who visited their home, ensured that everyone was fed and well, and balanced out her husband's vast appetites for creation and reform. She did all of this with empathy and panache.

There is a scene early on in the book about how Leela decided that Shivarama Karanth was the man she wanted to marry based on his beautiful hands. She proposed to him and he acceded in his own way. We all think Indian women, especially from the older generations, have been constrained by tradition and boundaries. Not so, as this memoir points out. Each of us contain 'multitudes,' to use Walt Whitman's term.

The best memoirs and biographies are both specific and universal. They offer a prism into their subjects but also into an ethos, a milieu. When I read the episode of Leela proposing, I remembered many other instances where women from conservative backgrounds surprised the world by 'being forward' in their approach. Most of us deal with stereotypes. Occasionally, a good book goes above them.

The book also portrays both Shivarama and Leela Karanth in all their complexities. The authors write about the tragedies that befell their family. They lost an elder brother, Harsha, very early on. Leela was later diagnosed as bipolar with alternating manic and depressive episodes. Karanth became enamoured with a much younger woman whom the authors call 'M' in the book.

Good biographies are cathartic for the readers and the

creators. They offer a glimpse into the inner and outer worlds of the subject. The best ones have a feeling and tone that allows the inner life of the subjects to fall off the page.

At the end of the book, I was fascinated by—and learned a lot about—the world that Leela and Karanth inhabited, about the many hues of their relationships, about their magnificent largesse of mind and spirit and the myriad small things that make up the landscape of Karnataka.

There are many types of biographies. The ones that I love the most are exactly like *Growing Up Karanth* that are written not as a worshipful hagiography but as gritty reality. The book portrays both Shivarama Karanth and his talented wife, Leela Alva Karanth, as fascinating, complicated human beings—each of them large-hearted and enormously talented in their own way, each with their own specific human frailties.

Most important of all, I saw in their lives shades of mine. I saw in their relationships people I had known. The feelings expressed in the book held a mirror to my own feelings. Isn't that what you want from a good book? To be able to lose yourself in it?

Growing Up Karanth will, no doubt, make many readers lose themselves in the book.

The Life and Death of Puneeth Rajkumar

Deepavali 2021 was a quiet and sombre one in Bangalore, not only because of Covid—it's long shadow is finally fading—but because of the sad and untimely death of Kannada superstar Puneeth Rajkumar at age 46.

'Look at these crowds,' said a hardened news reporter, filming the hundreds of thousands of weeping fans who had gathered. 'To touch so many lives so deeply is something amazing.'

The death of a Bollywood actor usually has this effect. But Puneeth Rajkumar seemed to wear his fame lighter than most. Perhaps, it was being born as the son of Rajkumar, a legend and icon in Karnataka. Perhaps, it was being the youngest son in a joint family of 30 people. Whatever the reason, the word that most people used to describe the 'power star' is 'humble'. You could see it in the movie clips that were playing on loop on Twitter after his death. There was a lovely one made by Hombale Films in which fans described how they used to watch Puneeth's films—first day, first show for many. As they talked, Puneeth quietly walked up behind them and ad libbed a phrase. 'Will you give me a ticket to see the movie with you?' he muttered. The woman fan turned to find her matinee idol standing behind her. He grinned, she screamed, they shook hands. You could see the delight in both parties.

Beyond the crowds, beyond the condolences from Prime Minister Modi, Sadhguru, Sanjay Dutt, Virendra Sehwag and from pretty much everyone in the Kannada film fraternity, one news item stood out—the fact that two fans died of heart attack when they heard about Puneeth's death. Now, a fan can die by suicide, as some did when they heard of superstar M.G.R's death in Tamil Nadu. But to die of a heart attack (of natural causes) requires you to be so linked to an actor emotionally that the grief of their passing is quite literally heartbreaking. This news, if true, tells us that Puneeth Rajkumar had an emotional resonance with his fans that few can equal.

Part of the reason for the shock is, of course, that Puneeth died tragically young—he was just 46. Also, the fact that he seemed really fit.

There was a fake message, ostensibly from Dr Devi Shetty, another denizen of Karnataka, that made the rounds during that time. It talked about people who are seemingly fit—like Puneeth was—and people who take exercising to the extreme—Puneeth allegedly died after working out for two hours in his gym. The message ends with the cheery call for moderation. *Eat what your ancestors did and exercise in moderation*, the message said. Fake as it was, the message resonated with many, including me, partly because all of us have lost friends and family who are ridiculously young during the pandemic, and not just because of Covid. The truth is that I personally know four people who died young in the last few years—because of a heart attack.

When people die young, the public post-mortem includes scrutinizing their lifestyle. Puneeth was known to be a fitness fiend, and suddenly, that was being called in question. A friend of mine cancelled a marathon because he was exactly Puneeth's age and his wife got freaked out by his 'extreme fitness', as she called it.

To me, the message in Puneeth Rajkumar's death was not about altering your lifestyle or your fitness routine. It wasn't even about practising moderation or being careful about what proteins, steroids or muscle relaxants you take. It was about the limits of human intervention and being humble enough to know what you can control.

People say that the only certain things are death and taxes. To that short list, I add pain. The one thing that lies in your future and mine is heartbreak. Some months ago, our family endured the loss of a young person—also because of a heart attack. It was horrible, unfair and heartbreaking. We are still reconciling with this loss—just as Puneeth's wife, Ashwini, and his two daughters, Vanditha and Drithi, will have to in the coming years.

It is easy to say that pain is and will always be part of the human condition but living through it is hard because pain hits you when you are least expecting it. How, then, does one make sense of it?

Well, our ancients tried to view pain as a pathway to the higher self. When the human ego is beaten, they said, the soul instantly recognizes this as an opportunity to shed what is no longer needed. When the heart is broken, the soul is released from its prior constellations. It begins the ancient process of dissolution, dismemberment and new life. Rebirth is not a comfortable process but a neccessary one.

Not all of us get to do this. Puneeth's family will have to.

GENDER

How Do Women Handle
Tech Companies?

I n Bangalore, where many of the top IT companies thrive, DE&I or diversity, equity and inclusion have become watchwords. How do women handle this?

At the Bangalore book launch of *Women of the Records* in 2021, musician Ricky Kej made an interesting observation, which, in turn, prompted fellow panelist Kiran Mazumdar Shaw to respond. Like many book launches, this too was a panel discussion held at the ever-popular Bangalore International Centre (BIC), and is available on YouTube.

Co-produced by Vikram Sampath and Ricky Kej, *Women of the Records*, highlights 25 women musicians—courtesans, *devadasis* and *tawaifs*—who were bold, broke the mould and led the way—all the qualities that we want and encourage in today's young women.

Bangalore is full of such women. Kiran Mazumdar Shaw is, of course, held up as the poster child but there are others. Entrepreneurs such as Meena Ganesh of Portea, Shubhra Chadda of Chumbak, Rashmi Daga of Freshmenu, Anisha Jain of Zivame and Shradha Sharma of YourStory are just a few women who have shattered the glass ceiling. Venture capitalists like Vani Kola, Ankita Vasishta and NassComm president, Rekha Menon, are also among these pioneering women.

Yet, there is one quality that women struggle with to this day, and that is power. Simply put, women have trouble owning and wielding power—perhaps not the ones in my list above, but many others. How do we address this issue? How do we teach women to wield power? One method is to model it for your children by being equal parents, or at least the kind where Mom doesn't defer to Dad. The other way is to change the system so that women get a chance to exercise power. This is what Kej was alluding to when he made his comment.

The panel discussion veered to the music industry of today. Kej said that in today's music world, there were a great many women professionals but they were all on the 'entertainment' side (singers, musicians) not the 'production' side (sound engineers, editors).

The production side had a male majority and men didn't want women to enter their field because they liked to hang out together late at night, smoke and drink together, he said. Women would only complicate this. This is true of most professions. Day traders in the stock exchange don't want women because things get complicated with the other sex. The way to change it is not by inserting one single woman into the fold but having a great many women in every field at every level of power.

'I think you need a quota system to ensure that women are equally represented,' said Kej. 'Anyone who says we don't need quotas is speaking from a place of privilege.' The audience clapped.

In response to Kej's comment, Kiran Mazumdar Shaw talked about DE&I being the buzzword in today's corporate world. She said that in her firm, she quietly incentivizes men to hire and include more women. Hire women for their potential and men for their competence, she said.

When I called him to talk about male privilege, Kej added that women, typically from the previous generation, underplay the gender card. *Look how far I've come*, they will say. *I am the Chief Excutive Officer (CEO) and I didn't need a quota.* But these women are the exception rather than the rule. Equally, they forget how many fires they had to jump through to get where they are. Privilege is a strange thing. Those who have it take it for granted and don't even realize its aura because they are surrounded by it. It is only when you are stripped away of your privileges that you feel the pain of those who don't have it.

I want to end with something that nobody talks about but is essential for empowerment. Gender balance is a numbers game. Diversity is not about including one token minority for them to 'feel' included. Today's corporate boards largely include women—but it is usually just one or two women among 12 men. This doesn't work to anyone's advantage—not women's, certainly, but in reality, not the firm's either.

We all know from personal experience how differently men behave when they are the sole man in a room full of women. Most men go quiet. Their manner becomes tense and muted. The same applies to women. Put a woman in a board room with only men and all its inherent tensions and think of whether she is going to voice her opinions. And please don't point at the token woman you know who is assertive in such a situation.

So, the next time someone asks you to be on a panel, check if there is some semblance of gender balance in it. If you are invited to be part of a jury, ask yourself: is the 10-person jury going to be comprised of only men? Book awards or any award with all-male juries tend to pick books written by men as the winner. Heck, women authors don't even make the shortlist. And this, in a gloriously heterogenous country such as ours, is not just plain wrong, it isn't sustainable.

Simply punting the issue back to women will not help. Men need to question each other's prejudices. They need to ask themselves this simple question: is this the milieu that I want my daughters or nieces to inhabit?

I should know. I am a classic example. I call myself a feminist and yet I have tremendous difficulty with being in a position of authority. When authority is thrust at me, I end up choosing the role of a peacekeeper rather than someone who calls the shots.

This plays out in small ways. I don't voice my opinions when I need to. I ask questions instead of making statements. I hate confrontation. I am not assertive. I value harmony over unpleasantness. I hate saying this but all of these qualities may make for a good *bahu* (daughter-in-law) but not for the self-professed strong woman that I am. Not all women are like me, thank God. They wield authority, hold power accountable, call the shots and take charge. But within each woman is what is now widely recognized as the 'imposter syndrome' or the feeling that you are faking it. Men have this too but to a lesser degree.

Every company or recording label that jumps on the diversity bandwagon typically goes all out to include a woman in a position of power. It skews my behaviour to be the sole woman in a room full of men, and I would wager that a single male in a room full of women would feel the same. Instead, if there is a modicum of gender balance, the conversation gets more robust as women feel comfortable voicing their opinions and everyone benefits.

Female Gang Violence in Bangalore

In a story worthy of a Rajinikanth thriller, two women—sisters-in-law—are the main players in a grisly gang murder.

On 24 June 2021, in the old Bangalore area of Cottonpete, former councillor, Rekha Kadiresh, who was slated to win the upcoming city council polls was hacked to death 17 times on a crowded street in broad daylight. Within a day, using CCTV footage, the Bangalore police arrested five people including Lambu Peter, who allegedly perpetrated the deed. They also arrested Mala Rajkannan, the ganglord of the area.

The plot gets thicker. Mala is the sister of Rekha's late husband, Kadiresh, a rowdy charge-sheeter who was hacked to death in 2019, in front of a temple. Kadiresh was the ward councillor of a small but vibrant area in Cottonpete. When the ward was set aside for female candidates, his wife, Rekha, took over and became a popular powerful player, negotiating deals for lucrative contracts with the garbage and construction mafia. She was going to contest and win the upcoming city council elections.

The trouble began when she tried to distance herself from her husband's family, all of whom migrated from Tamil Nadu and set up a powerful nexus of gangs that involved power, politics and the police. Mala wanted her own daughter-in-law to run for the seat that Rekha was contesting. When Rekha paid no heed to Mala's demands, Mala took out a 'contract' to get her killed. A power struggle between two hardened women—Mala and Rekha—is how this incident was described by the cops.

In press statements, the Cottonpete police said that Mala was a hard nut to crack because she has been in and out of jail for several decades, supplying marijuana to prisoners, dealing drugs, collecting bribes and wielding power.

This story is a far cry from how Kannada women are portrayed by the two giants of Kannada literature—Kuvempu and Shivarama Karanth. Both offered nuanced takes on women and how they wield power in their works. In his novels, *Kanooru Heggadathi* (The House of Kanooru) and *Malegalila Madumagalu* (The Bride of the Rainy Mountains), Kuvempu portrays women as creatures of circumstance.

Many of his heroines are caught as the daughters-in-law of feudal households. They slowly learn to make their way and get their way in their homes and society. With names like Seethe, Subbamma, Nagamma and Lakshmi, these women inhabit the fertile hills and valleys of Uttara or North Karnataka, as members of large households led by idealistic men. Their grasp of power is circumscribed and circuitous, not as fierce and clear-cut as women in political power in Karnataka today.

Karanth's leanings in his novels are generally pro-women, and more generally, pro-underdog. His novel, *Mai Mangala Suhiyalli* (The Woman of Basrur) speaks of the world of a courtesan and how she approaches sexuality without a shadow of prudishness.

The women who inhabit the worlds that both Karanth and Kuvempu described bear little resemblance to the rough and tumble politics of today's Karnataka and the raw belligerence of women politicians such as Shobha Karandlage.

It is no secret that the world has trouble with women wielding power. Culturally, Indians are more comfortable with the 'Rabri Devi model', where the husband is the power behind the throne.

In Bangalore, Ulsoor ward corporator, Mamatha Saravana had photos of her husband on election posters while she demurely folded her hands in a namaste. This is true all over Bangalore, where 50 per cent of the Bruhat Bengaluru Mahanagara Palike (BBMP) ward seats are reserved for women.

Against this backdrop, what should one make of women like Rekha and Mala? Do you have a sneaking admiration for them for being as 'bad' as the men? Or do you think of them as bad apples in a sea of demure *bharatiya naaris* (Indian women)?

When author Gillian Flynn wrote her blockbuster novel *Gone Girl*, in which the heroine is a scheming Machiavellian woman who frames her husband for murder, she said that she was tired of women being portrayed as neat and nice. She wanted to showcase heroines who were evil, fierce, scheming and had a killer instinct. She wanted to portray women as Kali instead of Lakshmi, in other words.

India has sanitized our women goddesses into benevolent Lakshmis and Saraswatis. Save for Kerala with its *Bhagavathi* cult and West Bengal, the fierceness and rage has been taken out of our women goddesses. Similarly, in real life, girls are raised to be tame in temperament.

The only way to counter this is to get more women into power, something that organizations like Shakti are attempting to do. Perhaps, if 50 per cent of the seats are occupied by women who actually wield power, then women like Rekha and Mala will not have to scramble for one seat.

Women, Work and the Pandemic

I t has been exactly four years since Covid-19 showed up in China and then in all of our lives. What are some memorable incidents or takeaways from it? Well, here's one.

In the throes of the lockdown, a strange event happened in our privileged apartment community in Bangalore. What was strange was how normal we thought it to be at that time.

Like most apartment buildings, ours banned all external help from entering the community unless their presence was absolutely essential. Covid was raging all through Bangalore. News of unnamed Covid-positive corpses being thrown into common burial sites made the rounds. We were all petrified of catching the virus. Household help for the elderly who lived in our building was allowed. But pretty much everyone else had to fend for themselves.

Then came a request. A young man wrote to the building committee asking if his cook could be allowed inside the building. He was a single working man, he said, and needed food. This was discussed. 'Tenant in Apartment 845 wants his cook to come, on alternate days at least, to cook for him,' was the gist of the discussion on the committee WhatsApp group. What was interesting was that most people in the 10-person committee, including the women, thought this was a normal request. Most were inclined to view this request favourably and allow the cook to 'help' the young man. 'Why should he starve?' was the view. Till one male member of the committee called him out. Why were we allowing the man to get a cook? Just because he was a man and couldn't cook for himself? In short, yes. That was the implicit bias that all of us were operating under. Men needed help cooking—nothing wrong with asking for support in that area.

The 'gendered impact' of the pandemic is well known. How do we take stock and make changes? For women, the pandemic was a source of more work and angst. Many of us were asked the question: has the lockdown opened the eyes of society to the 'multitasking capabilities' of women? It was meant as a compliment but was actually a curse. Thanks to the pandemic, women were forced to multitask more than ever—taking care of school-age children who were fed up of virtual classes, caring for elders who were driving them batty, enabling their husbands who usually tended to earn more money and were, therefore, necessary to bolster the household's finances. But what about the working woman herself? Who is going to enable her?

A harder and more neccessary stance might be the opposite. Yes, women can multitask but so can men. Thanks to being home-bound during the lockdown, some men found that they loved to cook and were terrific at it. Others found new purpose in helping their sons and daughters with art projects or math homework and took delight in being indispensable to their kids—'for a change', as one father said.

In my view, praising a woman's ability to multitask confines her to the stereotypical role of a caregiver and enabler, which, in turn, puts less pressure on men and society to admit that there is a problem in how women shoulder the burden of the household disproportionately.

Unlike at companies where jobs can afford to be specialized, households require flexibility, fluidity and agility—from all partners. If the pandemic has taught us anything, it is that men can be great moms—sending the kids off to school while their mother takes a Zoom call from work. Rather than celebrating the woman's ability to do more, I think it is time for society to celebrate the man's ability to do something inside the home. Men can and should step up and own up to household chores. It should no longer be acceptable to say, 'Oh, thanks to the pandemic, my son has learned to make tea.' As if making a simple tea deserves a crown.

India has among the lowest participation of women in the workplace. As a nation, our economy needs to bounce back from the Covid-19 recession. Supporting women in both roles—at home and the workplace—is not just good for the soul or society, it is great for the economy too.

Here is the thing: the pandemic only highlighted what we all knew. The fact that Indian society penalizes working women and does not support them was known even before the pandemic. It is what medical doctors call a pre-existing condition. The sooner corporates, governments and businesses act to nudge women back to the workplace, the better it is for India. Yes, a woman's place can be at home but also at the workplace, if women desire it to be so.

As for the man in my building, he could jolly well learn to cook for himself. It's about time. At least that is what the building committee decided, and we all lauded them for it.

PHILOSOPHY OF WEALTH

PHILOSOPHY OF NATURE

How Bangalore
Thinks about Money

'When did money become the be-all and end-all of Indian society?' the man asked. Which I thought was a bit rich (ahem, forgive the pun), given that we were tucking into a lavish Sunday brunch (priced at about ₹5,000 a pop) at the Four Seasons. So there we were, India's one-percenters talking about money and what it meant to us.

We were college friends who had seen each other rise and fall. We had come far from our humble beginnings. Our problem was one that is felt keenly in Bangalore where millionaires are made overnight: how could we enjoy the fruits of our hard work while ensuring that our kids stayed foolish, hungry and driven, to paraphrase Rashmi Bansal's terrific book?

Many middle-aged Indians who are successful professionals today have a similar trajectory. We have our 'unreserved compartment' stories. You know what I mean? Or maybe you don't. It is something that happens when you travel by Indian trains. There you are, after an ungainly undignified scramble, sitting on the upper-berth of the unreserved compartment, surrounded by sweaty bodies. In a scene worthy of a Kannada movie, you swear that you will never put yourself through this again.

Mostly you don't. Every professional I meet at Bangalore's great companies, be it Titan or Flipkart, have their 'origin tales' of how they struggled and succeeded. Equally, all of us, including me, now lead lives where we do everything we can so that our kids don't struggle. Our kids don't take public transport; they don't bike to buy vegetables and they never have to travel in the unreserved compartment on their trips home for vacation. Yet, we want them to stay grounded, hungry and driven, just as we were. The question is: can you get your kids to be hungry without letting them—quite literally—go hungry? How do you keep them grounded if you live in a glitzy high-rise?

Different parents take different strategies. My friend, Leo, for instance, flies business class when he is alone but travels economy whenever the family goes on vacation, so that his kids can learn the value of frugality. He also wants his kids to be ambitious and have a passion. 'We mostly define success and ambition as linked with wealth which I think is totally silly. Ambition to me is about going after what you want and working hard.'

As a parent, what are the two or three cardinal values that you would want to pass on to your children? For me, it would be frugality and grit but it could be different things for you. North Indians tend to use words like courage and determination. Frugality, I find, is valued mostly by South Indians (not including folks from Andhra or Telengana). I think it is because we have a certain uneasiness about wealth. We don't 'own' it emotionally, we have an inherent, and you could argue, well-placed suspicion about whether it will change our character.

Discussing frugality at the Four Seasons is a contradiction, you might say. But here lies the nuance. As adults, all of us want to enjoy our champagne brunch. Heck, we've earned it. But we don't want our kids to grow up thinking that this is their reality. We want them to earn it as well. So what is a parent to do? One option that we all came up with was to take our kids to Woodlands for outings rather than, say, to Zen at The Leela. Let them struggle, let them earn and then let them go out wherever they want was the rationale. Did we do it? Not really. In this day of helicopter parenting, kids tag along everywhere the parents go. All is not lost though.

Recently, Namu Kini, owner of the art gallery KYNKYNY, had put together a weekend market at Hatworks Boulevard, an oasis in the centre of Bangalore. Titled Uru Collective, it was a collection of homegrown brands—all leaning towards plant-based and sustainable solutions. What I saw at the market gave me hope. Most of the founders were Bangaloreans in their 20s and 30s. They came from privileged backgrounds. Yet, there they were, ambitious, if not hungry. They were following their passions, even if they didn't conform to their parent's traditional notions of success, which in India generally means medicine, engineering, law or accounting. These folks were entrepreneurs who followed their passions and principles. There was Angelo's Vegan cheeses, Asan menstrual cups, Bare Neccessities zero waste products, Huda Bar cereals and more. Look up Uru Collective's Facebook page for the full list of local brands.

Success has many models and each model has an expiry date. Today's youth prioritizes work–life balance, personal growth and happiness over brute force and climbing up the corporate ladder at the cost of pretty much everything. If you are a parent who has a child doing something counterintuitive, supporting them involves internalizing the hardest truth of all—our children are not our reflections. We need to understand that they are gloriously different individuals who march to a different beat. Ultimately, isn't that what successful parenting is all about?

Bangalore's Billionaires and Their Wealth

A funny thing happened as Bangalore was getting flooded with rainwater, making this city the laughing stock of the country and the world. Lakes breeched, storm-water drains leaked and multi-crore homes built on erstwhile wetlands had several feet of sewage and rain water inside. Viral videos of 'billionaires in boats' began making the rounds, much to the amusement of those in tenements.

What would you do if you are a billionaire who lives in Koramangala, Epsilon, 77 East and other elite real estate developments? Here in Bangalore, the press began getting phone calls from PR folks who wanted to 'clarify' that their billionaire clients—founders of said tech unicorns—did not live in those developments with their now flooded expensive homes.

A spate of conversation broke out on school groups about the hypocrisy of the new rich. 'They want to enjoy the trappings of wealth with their gazillion square foot homes but retain their middle class image,' tittered some. Which begs the question: why is new money uncomfortable with being named as rich? Why don't they own up to their newly-minted millionaire status instead of protesting so much? Is this desire to appear middle-class while you are actually a millionaire a South Indian thing? And is that a good or bad approach towards wealth, and for that matter, life?

The answer is a matter of personal choice, of course. If you suddenly come into wealth, you can either flaunt it or hide it. In

India, the stereotype is that North India, particularly Delhi, likes to 'show off' its wealth; while South India, particularly Chennai, likes to keep things quiet. Bangalore used to be a typical South Indian city with its emphasis on frugality and its suspicion of sudden wealth. But today, thanks (or no thanks depending on your point of view) to the growing number of immigrants, this city's equation with wealth is changing.

In Bangalore today, there are three strands. There is the old Bangalore which is quiet and values the ideas of frugality and discretion. Homes in Kingfisher Towers, several Benz cars and partying with the rich crowd is not for them. Early tech entrepreneurs who built companies such as Wipro and Infosys fall in this category. They live modest lives relative to their net-worth. The second category includes children of MLAs (Members of Legislative Assembly), real estate moguls, newly rich doctors and lawyers. They don't have their parent's hang-ups about money. 'My Dad grew up in a home where money was always viewed as tainted,' said one 20-year-old who drives a Porsche on Bangalore's pot-holed roads. For him, this whole idea of tainted wealth is a generational thing, a superstition and a hang-up that he has no patience with. If you have it, flaunt it, he says.

Bangalore's tech billionaires—the ones who call up newspapers to say, 'please don't print that I have bought a house for ₹50 crore; I only bought it because it needs to house my parents and in-laws too'—belong to the third strand. Generationally, they are closer to the Porsche-driving MLA's son. But they grew up in middle-class homes as sons of academics, around parents who taught them that struggle was a good thing. 'Money for money's sake' was never part of the discussion. Being wealthy was viewed with some suspicion because the assumption was that money, like power, would corrupt you. This is why Bangalore's newly-minted tech billionaires maintain a low-profile; at least some of them do. These are the folks who benefited from a public education system—whether it was from Indian

Institutes of Technology (IITs), Indian Institutes of Management (IIMs) or other such colleges—and absorbed its ethos. No matter what you say, India is still an ancient civilization where showing off is viewed with anxiety because it will attract *nazar* or the evil eye. You may belong to the top 0.1 per cent of the economy but you would still have heard the 'hide your wealth' messages.

The question is whether such a dichotomy is a good thing. Is it a good thing to have a ton of money and keep quiet about it or is that just hypocrisy? Is it a good thing to drive a Kia when you can afford a BMW? Is it a good thing to live in communities that aren't an 'address' or viewed as overly elite? Again, it depends on the person and his or her values.

The problem with flaunting your wealth and deifying the wealthy, which is what the press does, is that it inculcates a value system that is false. Today, if you go to Bangalore's top private schools and ask kids what they want to become, the answer is usually, 'I want to make a ton of money'. They are not sure how they will make the money or what career they will choose but they know that they want money. It is the goal rather than the byproduct, unlike what it was for the Bansals, Agarwals and Byju's who make up today's Bangalore. And all these tech billionaires, some of whom have children, are smart enough to recognize that there is something deeply wrong with wanting money as a life and career goal. That is, perhaps, why they are hiding their wealth, which to my South Indian mind, is a good thing.

The scary thing about wealth, particularly if you didn't grow up wealthy, is that it is like holding a tiger by the tail. It is terrific and exciting to catch it but you cannot predict the side-effects. Tech billionaires want to enjoy the fruits of their hard work without turning their kids into spoiled brats. This is the tightrope that Bangalore's tech icons are trying to walk. The sad thing, as one media colleague said, is that there are many 'wealthy wannabes' who are changing Bangalore into Delhi. Bangalore was about '*saaku*' or 'enough', they say. Now, it has become a '*beku*' or 'I want' culture without the ability or willingness to do the work that begets the want.

Life Takeaways from Bangalore's Groups

Every year, we ask ourselves and others about resolutions and takeaways. What changed in our lives? What remained constant? Just after Covid, this exercise took place in many of Bangalore's groups, both online and offline. It is interesting to see what one prioritizes after a particularly harsh pandemic. Even more interesting is the fact that so many of these have stayed and become part of the fabric of our lives.

Silk List, an online mailing list founded in Bangalore, had a discussion on this topic. So did many alumni reunions that I attended in person and virtually. I compiled the answers into categories and directives. Which one resonates with you?

- **Faith and hope restored:** Whether it is being awestruck by the frontline workers who showed up day after exhausted day, or the numerous small acts of kindness that we witnessed from our neighbours, all of us felt a twinge of hope in humanity. People gave to pet causes (migrant workers), charities (vaccine camps) and volunteered in their own ways.
- **Personal care:** This seems particularly universal. Freed of our commutes, lots of us developed self-care routines. We walked or ran every morning, restarted our yoga, pranayama and meditation practices, learned to cook at home and got healthier in the process.
- **Family time:** Since we were stuck at home, we planned dinner times with family. We had conversations about sexual

orientation and silliness, politics and memes with our siblings, friends, nieces and kids. We learned new ways of being.

- **Cloud kitchens:** Lots of restaurants became cloud kitchens. Lots of home cooks became caterers. Kappa Chakka Kandari, Go Native, Klaa Kitchen—all sent out comfort food to patrons all over Bangalore.
- **Creative collaborations:** Artists, dancers and musicians pivoted to the virtual world. They came up with new collaborations and ways to reach their audiences. Shaale.com set up master classes with musicians, mridangists and veena players. Now, music *rasikas* could learn *kunarkol* (chanting to the beats of a drum) or the *kanjira* (a tambourine like instrument) from the comfort of home. Many did.
- **Hobbies:** We dived into the things that we had been putting off. Bangalore has a thriving group that chants the Gita, plays bridge, does ikebana, goes birdwatching every week and does virtual music/antakshari.
- **Tackling big and deep projects that were put off:** With time on hand, people faced their inertia and decided to tackle the big, deep and difficult projects that they had put off forever. Some set a goal of reading a physical book for an hour a day. Some took up embroidery and knitting. Others made time to visit old relatives who they cordially disliked out of compassion. Still others wrote the business plan, launched a start-up, quit a job, joined an NGO, trekked in Kashmir or learned Kannada.
- **Enjoy small things:** We don't take life, living and breathing for granted any more. Thanks to enforced constraints, we took pleasure in small things—locally brewed Geist beer, Bengaluru Avarebele Mix from Postcard, warm croissants from Zed the Baker coupled with Begum Victoria's brie cheese, Araku or Kalmane coffee at home. We created terrace gardens and enjoyed a hot bowl of homemade bisi-bele bhaath with a nice dollop of Nei Native A2 ghee on top.
- **Splurge:** We took the acronym YOLO (You Only Live Once)

and the saying 'life is too short' to eat/drink/enjoy bad stuff to heart. So, we ordered rare orchids and tulips from the Flower Box. Since we couldn't travel, we bought expensive Burgundy wines, alongside local brands such as Grovers, KRSMA, Early Dark and SDU. We finally bought that Sailor fountain pen from William Penn or those Ganjam ruby earrings. We splurged on things we cared about.

- **Home improvement:** Lots of us painted our homes, bought that new teak wood chair from Vyom Studio or that cool antique trunk from Saanchi. We reupholstered our sofas with silk from Atmosphere and accessorized with playful toys from the Varnam Craft Collective.
- **Saved money:** Of course, we saved money. Where could we go? Well, some of us went to Karnataka's many wildlife sanctuaries, ranging from Dandeli to BR Hills to Kabini to Nagarahole. But, other than that, we couldn't go to restaurants or pubs, so we learned—some of us for the first time—to plan and invest our money.
- **Hotels and marriages took on new avatars:** Hotels offered staycations, private dining options and learned to pivot to become local, rather than global. Marriage ceremonies became small and virtual.

So, what was my Covid takeaway? It was learning to follow my bliss, which was being out in nature, ideally in a forest or at least in the woodlands, accompanied by expert naturalists who taught me how to see that spotted owlet camouflaged in the rain tree. I drank good wine, ate simple food and took pleasure in hugging vaccinated friends and family. Touch, you see, is an underrated comfort.

Bangalorean Secrets of Ageing Well

Deepa Mohan is a 66-year-old naturalist, theatre reviewer, punster, singer, mother and grandmother. She takes interested people all over Bangalore on nature outings called 'Deepa Mohan Walks'. She blogs about them too. To me, this combination of having a passion, a routine that includes physical activity and a hobby that keeps you engaged and surrounded by people is a great way to age. But hey, that's just me.

What is the secret of ageing well? I asked different questions to some thoughtful Bangaloreans.

How are you approaching ageing?

Prabha Chandra, psychiatrist: 'For me, at 60 years of age, it is about being authentic in everything I do and having meaningful connections and conversations with people of all ages. I still like to look good and pay attention to my appearance and attire but now it is more about what appeals to me rather than how I appear to others. Fortunately I have eager young students who keep me on my toes with their discussions and questions, so the mind stays active. I like to be on the move and physically active with my husband. We have a five-year-plan of covering as many wildlife national parks as we can!'

What does ageing mean to you?

Mohandas Pai, chairman, Manipal Global Education (MaGE) Services: 'When you get older, the days seem to end too fast. You realize that life is a complex unwieldy interaction between people. You learn to listen to other people's views, talk less, maintain relationships. Family becomes very important. Older role models have resilience, courage, a sense of spirituality and proportion and find peace within themselves. They also accept that, one day, they have to go and meet their maker. If you experience this kind of quiet acceptance, you find that it is the only real way to be. Ageing is a process where you try to make peace with yourself, find new relationships and new levels of happiness, quiet and solitude.'

Who is your role model with respect to ageing? What is the secret to ageing?

Rezwan Razack, managing director, Prestige Group: 'My role model is my older brother, Irfan. He is 69 but behaves and believes that he is 29. The secret of ageing is that you don't retire. You have to work till your last breath. I haven't missed work in 50 years because of sickness. The bottomline is that if you eat right, have a regimented lifestyle and work well, you won't have time to think of all your health problems. I have seen energetic happy people who hang up their boots. Within a short time, their thought process changes. The mind starts playing games. They complain of pains, headaches, chest congestion. Look at Biki Oberoi. He goes to work at 93. I plan to do the same.'

What does age mean to you?

Anindita Bhateja, physician: 'We hear this all the time—age is just a number. But it's not. Metabolic changes happen all the time. We slow down. But what we have on our side is experience, the ability to get in touch with our inner self and a stronger mind. If we train our minds, we can train our body. I am 52 years old. Today, I can do almost everything, albeit slowly. I can climb mountains, dive in the ocean, learn cycling, simply because I want to. So, go ahead and do what you want. Don't let age come in the way.'

Who is a Bangalorean who you think has aged well?

'Ravichandar V., director, BIC: My choice is former chief justice M.N. Venkatachaliah. He was a towering judicial personality with charming old-world values of decorum in sync with his constitutional responsibilities. Post-retirement, over the last 25 years, he has found a way to impart his considerable wisdom and deep reading to audiences in India and overseas. He epitomizes the traits of a generation gone by. They don't make many like him anymore! He has achieved this by staying engaged on issues of the day. He draws inspiration from our ancient way of life. His talk on 'what we owe each other' at the BIC drove home the symbiotic nature of our relationships which define us humans.'

What is special about Bangalore for ageing?

Prem Koshy, owner, Koshy's Café: 'Bangalore has always been called 'pensioner's paradise'. It was a sanctuary. You came to Bangalore and dropped all your *pangas* (issues). Bangaloreans have formed strong bonds across age groups. In Koshy's, I have seen this happening. There was always a culture of walking, cycling, running in our gardens and parks or rowing in our beautiful lakes. There is spirituality through the Sathya Sai Baba or Sri Sri Ravi Shankar ashrams. So we have it all. What I advocate is a few things: learn to breathe properly, have a zest for life, be in nature. Because the Universe is listening to every thought of yours. It only gives back what you put more energy into. So, share your love. And you will be loved in return.'

GUIDES AND ITINERARIES

Bangalore Guide

Bangalore already has many guidebooks. This certainly doesn't need to be one. But here are some recommendations that I give friends and family who visit the city.

Where to Sleep

The opulent Leela Palace with its arches and columns reflects the Indian design sensibility. Its proximity to Whitefield attracts multinational CEOs who fly in for the day.

The century-old Taj West End has a gracious colonial ambience. Winston Churchill, who began his career in a Bangalore regiment, stayed here. Richard Gere and George Soros have pondered philanthropy amidst its leafy environs here; while Sting has practised yoga within his reserved suite.

Conrad, in the centre of the town, attracted The Dalai Lama who stayed at this hotel overlooking Ulsoor Lake for a few days.

Le Meridien, opposite the golf course, attracts cost-conscious corporate folks. It has a nice business centre and offers a great South Indian breakfast at a slightly lower tariff.

Visiting government dignitaries stay at the sprawling Lalit Ashok. The Bangalore Literature Festival is held here.

The Indian cricket team stays at ITC Gardenia. Old Bangaloreans stay at its sister property, ITC Windsor.

Well-situated on M.G. Road is the sprawling yet serene Oberoi. Deepak Chopra and Goldie Hawn have stayed here, as did every person with the last name Toyota in the, well, Toyota motor company.

Media barons like the spare rooms and black-wood furniture at the hip Park Bangalore.

Near the highway, the Shangri-la is great for those who have business in central Bangalore but need to dash to the airport soon.

The JW Marriott overlooks the greenery of Cubbon Park.

Chancery Pavilion is centrally located. It has some great amenities like a 24-hour check-in and check-out. This means that jetlagged international travellers arriving at 4.00 a.m. can check in right away instead of waiting till noon.

Where to Eat

These are old favourites. Go to the 'Food' section of the book for other theme-related suggestions.

If you are wearing black and hankering after a risotto, you'll fit right into Alto Vino in Whitefield, which serves flavourful Italian food to a youngish crowd.

The Royal Afghan does fantastic kebabs in an al fresco setting.

Hugely popular with locals, Mainland China serves dishes that combine Indian and Chinese cuisine.

If you want to score with locals, tell them you want to dine at MTR. It is an institution in Bangalore. It doesn't take reservations, so you'll have to queue up for the rich, tasty South Indian food.

Set in a lovely Moorish bungalow, Olive Beach, an outpost of Mumbai's acclaimed Olive, attracts a stylish crowd and magazine editors. Try the risotto.

Rim Naam, at The Oberoi, has great Thai food, including stir-fried squid with cashews and lemongrass.

If you want a taste of South India in a posh relaxed setting, go to Dakshin at ITC Windsor for its thali (plated) dinners. The Royal Afghan serves Northwest Frontier cuisine—a favourite of President Clinton.

Citrus, at The Leela Palace, has the best Sunday brunch in town. Book way in advance.

Falak, at the Leela Bharatiya City, does fine-dining Indian with flair.

Copitas at the Four Seasons has won the best hotel bar two years in a row. After a drink, go to Far & East, its Pan-Asian restaurant for well-made food in a stylish, romantic setting.

Honore Bakery, Loafer & Co and Lavonne make excellent bread, muffins, croissants and pastries.

Lupa serves Mediterranean food in the heart of M.G. Road.

The Three-Hour Tour

Call Bangalore Walks for a personalized and customized three-hour tour of Bangalore. If you just want a break, you can't do better than take a walk through the 240-acre Lalbagh Botanical Gardens. Created in 1760, these gardens boast a stunning variety of flora, fauna, birds and humans. Surrounding the orchid-filled Glass House are wide red-sand paths and expansive lawns.

Another place to while away a couple of hours is Blossom Book House. One of the best English-language bookstores in the country, this cluttered independent bookstore is notable for its bountiful India and foreign collections—from history to cookbooks to fiction. The staff will promptly procure almost anything you don't see on the shelves.

Spas

Bodycraft does good facials. Rejuve, at The Lalit Ashok, has a colour therapist who aims to balance your energy using prisms and gemstones. SOUKYA, an hour away from Bangalore, has half- and full-day packages that include a hot-stone massage and lunch. The Spa, at The Leela Palace, is a great place to get an aroma massage. Jiva Spa, at Taj West End, organizes yoga classes. The spas at The Ritz-Carlton, J.W. Marriott and Conrad are perhaps the best in town.

Shopping

Government-owned Cauvery Handicrafts Emporium is a one-stop shop for souvenirs—from sandalwood idols to incense to handicrafts. Nearby, P.N. Rao Tailors has been in business for generations and can deliver a bespoke suit in 24 to 48 hours. Crossword, Blossom and Gangarams are good bookstores. The Vintage Shop has lovely curios and will ship purchases abroad.

What to Do in an Hour or Three in Bangalore?

If you had one, three or five hours to explore Bangalore, what would you do?

Called the 'Silicon Valley of India', Bangalore sits atop the Precambrian Deccan Plateau at 3,000 ft above sea level. Its great weather, genteel people and flowering trees make this 'Garden City' amongst the most cosmopolitan in India. These itineraries take you through colourful markets, colonial-era museums and buzzing brewpubs. So, what do you do when:

You Have an Hour to Shop

Buy handwoven scarves or handcrafted leather goods.

- Walk to 1 MG Mall to experience global and local brands.
- Buy an emergency toy for kids back home at Hamley's.
- Take home souvenirs from some of India's finest brands like Fabindia and Kama.

While you can rush in for that emergency Estee Lauder lipstick, Clark's shoes, Body Shop perfume, M&S or H&M T-shirts, far more interesting are the Indian outlets in the mall.

Kama Ayurveda, feted by Vogue and Tatler, sells high-quality face creams, body washes and cleansers based on the 5,000-year-old tradition of Ayurveda. Buy the saffron-based *kumkumadi* scrub, fragrant and spill-proof hair oils or rose-and-jasmine scented hair cleansers.

Fabindia, beloved amongst Indians and the diaspora for its kurta–pyjamas, is a hugely successful brand, selling Indian clothes, scarves, stoles, bedsheets, cutlery, organic food and everything in between.

Insider Tip: On the road adjoining Hotel Conrad that goes into Ulsoor Market sits a man with physical disabilities who has been selling coconut water at the corner of Ulsoor road for decades.

You Have One Hour and You Want to Be Active

Go for a run around Ulsoor Lake. Follow it up with a yoga session.

- Go for a run around one of Bangalore's largest lakes.
- Take your binoculars and get up close to waterfowl.
- Watch neighbourhood women bargaining and buying fresh vegetables.

Ulsoor, once called Halasuru or 'Village of Jackfruits', is one of the oldest neighbourhoods in the city. The Ulsoor Lake was built by Kempe Gowda I after whom Bangalore's Kempegowda International Airport is named. Locals throng Ulsoor Lake in the mornings between six to ten o' clock to jog, walk, stretch or walk their dogs. Birdwatchers can bring binoculars to see brahminy and black kites, cormorants, wagtails, kingfishers, pond herons, white egrets and other waterfowl. They also rue the water quality of the lake, which goes through ups and downs in terms of cleanliness.

You Have One Hour and You Want to Experience Spirituality

Visit the Divine Trinity: A church, a temple and a gurudwara.

- Visit a 1,000-year-old temple in Ulsoor.
- Visit one of Bangalore most iconic military churches.

- Visit the most important gurudwara where Sikhs come to worship.

The Someshwara temple has an interesting story. Legend has it that Kempe Gowda, the chieftain who built Bangalore, fell asleep under a tree in the area. The Lord appeared in his dream and told him to build a temple using buried treasure, which he did. Epigraphs on the temple walls show a layered history, dating back through the centuries. Lovers of heritage architecture will enjoy the variety of styles within the temple.

Built in 1851 by the East India Company in English Renaissance style, the Holy Trinity Church is the largest military church in South India. With lovely stained glass windows, carved statues and inscriptions about British soldiers, the church seats 700 people. Services continue to this day, mostly in Tamil.

The Sikh Gurudwara of Ulsoor welcomes people of all faiths and is known for its free Sunday feast called langar, where devotees volunteer to cook and serve. In the gurudwaras and Hindu temples, modest attire is necessary. Avoid shorts or sleeveless T-shirts. Visitors must cover their heads in all gurudwaras. Headcovers are provided at the gurudwara entrance.

You Have an Hour in Central Bangalore and You Want to Experience a Bazaar

Wander through a typical and ancient Indian bazaar.

- Smell fresh jasmine garlands.
- Taste some fresh quintessentially Indian fruits like custard apple, *sapota* (sapodilla) and amla.
- Bargain for camphor and incense.

Ulsoor market is both an ancient and a living market. Locals throng the market to buy banana leaves, strings of jasmine and marigold and coconuts. Walking through the congested streets of the market requires a tolerance for chaos, crowds and the odd cow. Tiny by-lanes lead into bazaars selling vegetables, fruits, and prayer items like camphor, fresh turmeric, vermilion powder, mango and betel leaves. Men and women sell fruits, flowers and vegetables on wandering trolley carts. Tiny shops sell all manner of kitsch.

The Indian National Trust for Art and Heritage (INTACH) Bangalore does excellent heritage walks on a periodic basis. Details of their 'Parichay' heritage walks are available on their website at www.intachblr.org.

You Have an Hour and You Want to Get Fit

Go to Cubbon Park for communal exercises.

- Do tai chi in the park.
- Join a group doing yoga and breathing exercises.
- Pet a dog.

Named after an Englishman and built during the rule of the Mysore Maharajah, this 300-acre park is a magnet in the morning. Go at seven o' clock to join groups practising yoga, tai chi and breathing exercises. Park your car at the Cubbon Road entrance near the Metro station. Walk in and you cannot miss the group classes. Otherwise, simply walk or jog through and enjoy the large rain trees, the dog walkers, birds and the serially flowering trees like the bright yellow tabebuia, millingtonia, jacaranda, laburnum and flaming red gulmohar. Otherwise, you can laugh with or laugh at the laughing clubs and guffaw your heart out.

You Have One Hour and You Have Your Children with You

Visit the oldest bakery in Bangalore.

- Have a rose cookie.
- Try a flaky flatbread stuffed with sweet cheese.
- Chew on a mutton cutlet.

Founded in 1902 and still run by the same family, Albert Bakery is only open from three to nine o' clock. Most of the good stuff—the khova naan, which is a flaky flatbread stuffed with sweet cheese; the chicken and mutton puffs and pumpkin custard sell out early. Also in Frazer Town is Thom's Bakery & Supermarket, famous for its rose cookies and fruit cakes. Down the road is St Francis Xavier's Cathedral—one of Bangalore's largest churches.

Several independent companies, such as Unhurried and Bangalore Magic, do food trails of different parts of Bangalore.

You Have One Hour for Unusual Shopping near M.G. Road

Buy some incense in an ashram, a silk saree or a funky dress.

- Get a flavour of Pondicherry.
- Visit a saree boutique.
- Have a coffee.

Come down Annaswamy Mudaliar Road that borders Ulsoor Lake. An outlet of the Sri Aurobindo Ashram of Pondicherry, this verdant quiet space is great for buying incense, paper goods, fragrant candles and perfumes. There is parking available on site—a luxury in Bangalore. Further down the road is Ambara, an old boutique with a well-curated collection of silk sarees, tops, jewellery, candles and plants. Housed in a heritage bungalow with red floors and curving balconies, the in-house café is good for a spot of tea, coffee or a light lunch.

You Have One Hour with Family

Visit a military museum.

- Walk into a lush army cantonment.
- See sepia-toned photographs and memorabilia of the Indian army.

This takes a bit of planning but if it works, you will have succeeded in going where few Bangaloreans get to tread. Open only on weekdays by appointment with an army commandant, the Madras Sappers Museum and Archives lies inside a lovely army cantonment. The Madras Sappers are the oldest army corps of engineers in the Indian army and the ones that devised the Bangalore torpedo, used to this day in the US, UK, Israel and other places to breach barbed wire obstacles. Today, the free museum can be accessed with special permission from the army. Military buffs can duck in and out in half an hour.

Call +91 9611927256 and speak to the lieutenant colonel in charge to get permission. Hours: Between 9.00 a.m to 3.00 p.m. on weekdays. Details can be found on the museum website.

You Have Three Hours for Good Food

Enjoy a Bangalore biryani.

- Try a gently spiced coal-cooked biryani.
- Ride in an autorickshaw.
- Smell some roses.

Taj Hotel in Shivajinagar looks nothing like the monument after which it is named. This crowded neighbourhood is best accessed by an autorickshaw, if you are up for the ride. The service is fast, the cooking slow. The biryani gets its fragrance from the short-grained rice that is cooked over coals and the melt-in-the-mouth mutton or chicken; and it is lightly spiced with cloves, cardamom and cinnamon. Vegetarians and vegans can opt for a masala dosa at Hotel Ashoka nearby.

Work off your food or work up an appetite by walking through Russell Market. Housed in a colonial-style building, this market sells fruits, vegetables, fish, fresh-cut meats, and best of all, fragrant rose, tuberose, marigold and jasmine garlands that are strung by men with lightning hands. Great for photo buffs.

You Have Three Hours for Shopping

Visit the street where all of Bangalore comes to shop.

- Buy bangles, bindis, baubles and breakfast all in one shot.
- Tailor or buy traditional Indian kurtas or saree blouses.
- Punctuate this with fresh-cut guavas.

Commercial Street, the saying goes, sells everything except your mom and dad. Ten minutes by car from the nearby hotels, you can spend an hour or five over here buying things you didn't know you needed—like peacock fans, wooden drums, puppet strings and pots from vendors who trawl the streets. Shops open only at 11.00 a.m.; and the best ones open at noon, so there's no need to rush. Wander through the alleys and you will find tiny shops selling cheap costume jewellery, glass bangles, bindis (a coloured mark or sticker that Indian women wear on their forehead), sandals and hair clips. Men on bicycles peddle baskets of fresh guavas. Those with strong stomachs can have the fruits cut right there (wash them with bottled water if you like) and have them with salt and red chili powder.

Several shops like Lal Silk Creations and Salonee Silks N Cottons sell silk and cotton fabrics by the yard. For a quintessential Indian experience, buy a metre or two of fabrics and ask the shop to guide you to a tailor down the street. Many stitch a kurta or blouse (for sarees or other clothes) in a day, or if pushed, in several hours. Designing a blouse or kurta while sitting across a tailor is something every Indian has experienced.

Another option is to visit Brigade Road which has similar ethos.

You Have Three Hours for Art and Culture

Visit a museum that once was a home.

- Wander through the old rain trees that define Bangalore.
- Commune with art.

The NGMA is housed in a lovely white mansion that once was the home of the Velu family, whose descendents still live in the area. It was once called 'Manikyavelu Mansion' (yes, quite a mouthful) after the patriarch. Today, it has a rotating roster of shows and exhibits that include global, national and Indian artists. The manageable size of the museum means that you can duck in and out in an hour while en route to the airport, or spend three hours wandering through its quiet rooms and verdant yard. Visit the small temple next door that is dedicated to the Hindu monkey god, Hanuman.

You Have Three Hours with Family

Visit a children's bookstore, a cartoonist and a park.

- Visit Bangalore's best children's bookstore.
- Laugh over some cartoons depicting Bangalore of yore.
- Walk through a neighbourhood park or have a coffee.

Lightroom Book Store, tucked away in Cooke Town, is Bangalore's best children's bookstore. Here, you will discover books that are not found anywhere in India. Some are not to be found anywhere else in the world. Curated by a passionate bibliophile, Lightroom is a haven for tired and cranky children (and adults) who can browse or buy picture books on Indian folk art, mythology as well as good story books.

Apaulogy is the gallery of Paul Fernandes, Bangalore's beloved cartoonist. Wander through his wonderfully whimsical and compact gallery to learn about and laugh at Bangalore through the ages.

Richards Park epitomizes the neighbourhood parks that used to dot the city. Walk through the park to Corner House Ice Creams or Happy Belly Bakes for ice cream and cookies. On the way back, stop at The Cinnamon Store, a well-curated boutique that has a café as well as stores selling contemporary Indian sarees (Raw Mango), lovely embroidered kurtas, yoga apparel and home wear.

You Have Three Hours for Activities or Adventure

Walk or run among trees that were sourced from all over the world.

- Take a nature walk in Lalbagh.
- Stand on one of Bangalore's oldest rock formation.
- Eat at an iconic restaurant.

Lalbagh, beloved of Bangaloreans, is a 240-acre park that—depending on time of day—will take you 15 minutes or 45 to get to. Like most parks, dawn and dusk are its peak hours for running, walking or people-watching. Two men—a Sultan and a German—were responsible for creating this park. Tipu Sultan hired Gustav Krumbiegel, a German horticulturist, to source trees from all over the world. Nature buffs will recognize these fruiting and flowering trees from Madagascar, Peru and Australia. Birdwatchers can look for egrets, spotted owlets, barbets, ducks and dozens of other species—carry your binoculars. Amateur geologists or mere rock-climbers can clamber over a rock formation that is 3.4 billion years old, dating back to Precambrian times. After the cacophonous traffic, Lalbagh is just a nice place to decompress.

Most people walk or run through Lalbagh and then have a coffee or breakfast at the iconic Bangalore eatery, MTR. Try the soft spongy rava idlis or the crisp dosas.

You Have Three Hours for Shopping

Visit a contemporary galleria and have a craft beer after.

- Buy or browse through local and global luxury brands.
- Buy jewellery.
- Have an Indian, Pan-Asian, Mediterranean or Mexican meal.

UB City is where affluent Bangalore comes to shop, eat and drink. Global luxury brands like Ferragamo, LVMH and Tumi have their stores here, so do Apple and Samsung. The café level has a number of popular and good restaurants. Pick a cuisine and walk in. The high footfall (and rents) ensure quality.

More interesting, perhaps, are the luxury Indian brands that dot this neighbourhood. Across the street in a discreet beige building is Bangalore's best jewellery store—Ganjam Jewellers. Walk in to see exquisite diamond, gemstones and gold, set in amazing—and expensive—designs. If Umesh Ganjam, the owner, is at hand, pepper him with questions about the heritage of India—a topic which he is passionate about. Round the corner from UB City are Forest Essentials for fragrant Indian skin and hair potions and Good Earth which curates and sells some of India's most innovative designs and products.

The area is also home to buzzing bars, brewpubs and stand-alone restaurants. Go to The Biere Club for beer, Sunnys, Toscano or Fava Bistro for excellent Mediterranean, and Bootlegger or Skyye bar for cocktails.

You Have Three Hours for Art and Culture

Listen to a concert or attend a dance performance.

- Listen to live music.
- Dance the night away.
- Shop for clothes.

Bangalore was once called 'Pub City,' for its drinking culture. The 100 Feet Road in the Indiragar neighbourhood is a hub of activity at night. Go after dinner for live music, poetry readings, and if you are in the mood for it, dancing. Take 5 is a music bar that obviously alludes to Dave Brubeck and has live music. Humming Tree does music but also poetry and stand-up comedy. Toit is a brewpub with a variety of draught beers. Walk into any of the high-end shops that line the road for clothes. Dance the night away at any of the bar/lounges on 12th Main Road.

You Have Five Hours for Food

Sample Bangalore's street food and visit a flower market.

- Walk down food street and sample local delicacies.
- Buy or photograph the region's biggest flower market.

Not for the faint of heart (or feet), this requires walking through jostling crowds. Food Street or Thindi Bheedhi comes alive when the sun goes down but is open throughout the day. Broadly akin to Singapore's hawker centres, this version is less organized, and—it must be said—less clean. This is not to say that it is unsanitary. Given that most of the food is cooked or fried, visitors should be okay. Sample sweet *holige* that is made with unprocessed sugar or jaggery, ghee and patted into a flat circle. Have a masala dosa made to order in minutes. Try a Congress bun, named after the political party, at V.B. Bakery. Try fried savoury snacks and chips called chaklis at Sri Vasavi Condiments. Sip some coconut water or carry a bottle. If nothing else, enjoy the theatrics of sizzling food, shouted orders, bargaining vendors and bemused tourists.

The nearby K.R. Market is where jasmine, marigolds and roses from the region come to be sold in bulk to florists across the city. Witness and photograph the riot of colours and designs with which the flowers are hand-tied into garlands. You cannot bottle their fragrance, alas, but you can buy a tuberose garland to take to your room.

You Have Five Hours for Wellness

Experience a holistic health centre frequented by the King of England.

- Consult with a homeopath, naturopath or an ayurvedic doctor.
- Experience a massage.
- Enjoy medicinal gardens followed by an organic vegetarian meal.

An hour outside Bangalore is SOUKYA, a world-class holistic health centre that has been visited by Archbishop Desmond Tutu; the King and Queen of England, Charles and Camilla; and Middle Eastern royal families. Headed by Dr Issac Mathai who has a thriving homeopathic practice in London and the Middle East, the verdant property which is lined with pink bougainvillaea has organic gardens, a restaurant, rooms and halls for massage, meditation and yoga. They make ayurvedic massage oils in-house using herbs grown on the property, thus compounding their effect or so one presumes. Have the concierge make an appointment and get out of the city for half a day.

You Have Five Hours for Action & Adventure

Trek to a spot where an iconic Bollywood film was made.

- Go trekking in a place where Sholay was made.
- Dip your feet in the Kaveri.

Mention the name '*Sholay*' to any Indian and they will smile. This iconic Bollywood film about friendship and revenge was shot in Ramanagara, an hour outside Bangalore. Hikers and rock climbers from Bangalore congregate here on weekends. Find a trekking group using the India Hikes portal if you are in the city on a weekend. Or else, hire a guide to take you there. There are treks of varying lengths—ranging from one hour to several.

If hiking is not your thing, drive on to Srirangapatna, where the river Kaveri—also an icon that is fought over by two neighbouring states—flows through. Dip your feet into its waters, considered holy by Indians.

You Have Five Hours for Shopping

Jayanagar and Basavanagudi are old neighbourhoods where the original Kannada inhabitants of Bangalore live. The late, great author, R.K. Narayan, combined Basavanagudi and

Malleshwaram—two iconic Bangalore neighbourhoods—to come up with his fictional town of Malgudi, where all his books are set. The Jayanagar 4th Block Shopping Complex is a bustling kitschy market that sells condiments, powders and Hindu puja-ritual objects. The surrounding area is full of shops. Visit Angadi Silks for, well, silk sarees; its swanky sister shop, Angadi Galleria, is across town. Go to Basava Ambara, opposite Krishna Rao Park, for its curated curios, clothes and jewellery. Gandhi Bazaar is an Instagram-friendly and fragrant flower, fruit and vegetable market. Wander through to another iconic restaurant, Vidyarthi Bhavan, just to see the waiters carry a line of plates containing crisp dosas on their hands

You Have Five Hours with Family for Activities or Adventure

Visit a national park and look at white tigers.

- Go on a herbivore safari.
- Visit a butterfly garden.
- Watch Indian conservation at work.

Banerghatta Biological Park is about one and a half hours away from central Bangalore. It is a great place for nature lovers and families to visit. Go on an-hour-long safari to see deer, *gaurs* (Indian bison), tigers, lions, leopards and bears. There are butterflies and birds aplenty, so carry binoculars. Birdwatchers can join the Bangalore birding community's free Sunday birding trips.

Conclusion

I have lived in Bangalore for almost 20 years. It is the place where I learned how to live, love, laugh and cry. It is where I raised my children and cared for my elders. It is where I learned the ways of India, both obvious and subtle—how to bargain and when to not, how to deal with the staring, how to cross the street amidst traffic, how to shop for vegetables, how to answer pointed specific questions about what my salary was and how much my apartment cost.

It has been a terrific ride to live in India and in this city.

This is my love letter to the place that I now call home.

I love you, Bangalore! *Ee pustaka Namma Bengaluru-goskara!*

Acknowledgements

This book would not have happened without the unstinting support of Sukumar Ranganathan, editor-in-chief of Hindustan Times. Ever since I began writing for HT Media, beginning with *Mint Lounge's* first issue in February 2007, Sukumar has been my editor and supporter. When I quit writing the 'The Good Life' column for *Mint Lounge*, he moved me to *Hindustan Times* to write a column for *HT Brunch* called 'This Indian Life.' During Covid, thanks to downsizing, that column was stopped. Sukumar then asked me to write a column about Bangalore. That is how this book began.

Living and working in Bangalore has been a pleasure and a relief, given how welcoming this city is of immigrants like me. Most of the people who influenced my stay in Bangalore are already mentioned in this book. Here are a few other institutions who have enlivened our lives here:

Institutions like Takshashila, Centre for Wildlife Studies (CWS), Natya Institute of Kathak & Choreography (NIKC), the Neev Literature Festival (NLF) and the Bangalore International Centre (BIC) have helped me understand the many facets of the city. Informal groups have also made this city immensely pleasurable. They include Author Evenings hosted in a private home, the Salon of Ideas which is a loose informal group of friends, Adda Ladies, The Wine Connosieurs (TWC), Bangalore Wine Club (BWC), Koramangala Lunch Group (KLG) and the Crafts Council events.

Friends make a city into a home. In that, I am richly blessed. I have learned from and enjoyed the company of many

Bangaloreans—too numerous to mention here.

Rupa was my first publisher in India. I am delighted to return to the fold with this book. My thanks to my editor, Dibakar Ghosh, for our conversations and his stewardship of the book; and to Anam Kazmi, Smita Mathur and Aditi Mehrotra, who meticulously copy-edited this book and improved it greatly.

This book is dedicated to my brother and sister-in-law, Shyam and Priya Sunder. Together with their children, Sangeeta and Harsha, they were our first home in Bangalore. We stayed with them for close to two years when we first moved to India from Singapore. Later, we bought our own apartment in their building. They have been guides and beacons during our early years. Now, we have settled into a comfortable routine as neighbours and family. Bangalore, or Bengaluru, would not have been 'home' without them and therefore, this book is dedicated to them.

Further Reading

While writing this book, I benefitted greatly from reading these books and I highly recommend them to anyone who wants to understand this gracious and genteel city.
Caveat: This is an incomplete and personal list.

1. *Bangalore Through the Centuries* by M. Fazlul Hasan: A magisterial account of Bangalore's history along with rare glimpses into telling anecdotes.
2. *The City Beautiful: A Celebration of the Architectural Heritage and City-Aesthetics of Bangalore* by T. P. Issar: This book by the late retired IAS officer showcases the many facets of this beautiful city written from the point of view of an immigrant who (like me) grew to love the city.
3. *Blossoms of Bangalore* by T.P. Issar: A must-read for anyone who enjoys the greenery of Bangalore.
4. *Monkey Tops: Old Buildings in Bangalore Cantonment* by Elizabeth Staley: For anyone who wants to know how these architectural details of the city came about.
5. *Bangalore: A Century of Tales From City to Cantonment* by Peter Colaco: Richly illustrated by Paul Fernandez, this book can be devoured in an afternoon.
6. *The Bangalore Detectives Club* by Harini Nagendra: A charming tale that drips with nostalgia and fun.
7. *Past & Curious: Forty Tales of Good Old Bangalore* by Stanley Carvalho: A rollicking read.
8. *Bangalore's Lalbagh: A Chronicle of the Garden and the City* by Suresh Jayaram: About Bangalore's best-known gardens.

9. *Beladide Noda Bengaluru Nagara* by Janaki Nair: It features lovely old maps and photos.
10. Aliyeh Rizvi's lovely blog about Bangalore called *A Turquoise Cloud* which can be accessed at www.aturquoisecloud. wordpress.com